CW00672008

The
Connell Guide
to
Shakespeare's

Othello

by
Graham
Bradshaw

Contents

Introduction

With the exception of *Hamlet*, *Othello* is Shakespeare's most controversial play. It is also his most shocking. Dr Johnson famously described the ending as "not to be endured", and H.H. Furness, after editing the Variorum edition of the play, confessed to wishing that "this tragedy had never been written". No play in performance has prompted more outbursts from onlookers: there are many recorded instances of members of the audience actually trying to intervene to prevent Othello murdering Desdemona.

It is a more domestic tragedy than *Hamlet*, *King Lear* or *Macbeth*, and it is the intimacy of its subject matter which gives it its dramatic power. "*Othello* is a faithful portrait of the life with which we are daily and hourly conversant," wrote one anonymous Romantic critic. "Love and jealousy are passions which all men, with few exceptions, have at some time felt; the imitation of them, therefore, finds an immediate sympathy in every mind."

Othello has also prompted more critical disputes than any other play except *Hamlet*. How could the hero possibly believe his wife had been unfaithful within a few days of their marriage? Is the marriage properly consummated (as it is usually assumed to be)? Is Othello a noble hero or is he really just a self-deluded egotist? And in this play about a disastrous inter-racial marriage, how important is the whole issue of race? Is the play itself racist?

This book looks at what *Othello* is really about and why it has such power to move us. It seeks to resolve the disputes which have taxed critics, or at least to resolve them as far as the text will allow. It aims to offer a clear, authoritative and fresh view of *Othello,* while taking account of the many fascinating insights other critics have had into the play in the four centuries since it was written.

THE CHARACTERS

OTHELLO, *a Moor, General in the Venetian Army*

DESDEMONA, *his wife*

CASSIO, *his lieutenant*

IAGO, *the Moor's ensign*

EMILIA, *wife of Iago*

BIANCA, *mistress of Cassio*

RODERIGO, *in love with Desdemona*

THE DUKE OF VENICE

BRABANTIO, *A Venetian senator, Desdemona's father*

GRATIANO, *his brother*

LODOVICO, *his kinsman*

MONTANO, *former Governor of Cyprus*

Senators of Venice, Gentlemen of Cyprus, Musicians, Officers, A Clown in Othello's household, A Herald, A Sailor, A Messenger, Soldiers, Attendants and Servants

A summary of the plot

Act One

Like so much of the play, the first scene takes place at night. Iago, Othello's personal ensign, complains that he has been passed over as Othello's lieutenant in favour of Cassio. He and Roderigo taunt Brabantio, a Venetian senator, telling him his daughter Desdemona has eloped with Othello, the general of the Venetian army and a Moor. Othello and Brabantio appear before the Venetian Senate, and Othello describes how he courted and won Desdemona. When she enters and takes her husband's side against her father, Brabantio is forced to accept the marriage. Othello is posted to Cyprus, to defend the island against a threatened Turkish invasion. Desdemona is allowed to accompany him. Roderigo, in love with Desdemona, despairs. Iago persuades him to follow her to Cyprus, and suggests he will be able to cuckold Othello.

Act Two

The remainder of the play takes place in Cyprus,
over two nights and a day. We learn that the Turks
were indeed about to invade, but that a storm wiped
out their fleet. (This is the point at which Verdi
begins his opera, *Otello*.) Desdemona arrives in
Cyprus, escorted by Iago, his wife Emilia, and
Roderigo. Othello, delayed by the storm, arrives
shortly afterwards and greets Desdemona lovingly.
Iago persuades Roderigo that Desdemona loves
Cassio, and incites him to challenge Othello's
lieutenant. In Act Two, Scene Three, a dramatic
tour de force which spans an entire night, he plies
both Roderigo and Cassio with drink and sets
them fighting. Montano, the island's former
governor, becomes involved and Cassio wounds
him. Othello is called from his chambers to quell
the riot, and Iago tells him that the quarrel was
begun by Cassio. Othello dismisses Cassio. Iago
advises Cassio to ask Desdemona to plead his case
with Othello (which will make it easier for Iago to
suggest Desdemona is Cassio's lover).

Act Three

Othello comes upon Cassio asking Desdemona
for her help. Iago hints to Othello that Cassio and
Desdemona may be lovers. Desdemona appeals to
Othello to help Cassio; he agrees: "I will deny thee
nothing." Iago then goes to work on Othello in
the so-called "Temptation Scene", suggesting that

Desdemona has been unfaithful. Desdemona returns briefly, accidentally dropping her handkerchief – the handkerchief was her first present from her husband. Emilia picks it up and hands it to Iago. Othello, growing ever more jealous, demands that Iago give him proof of Desdemona's infidelity. Iago tells him that she has given the handkerchief to Cassio. When Desdemona renews her pleas on behalf of Cassio, Othello asks for the handkerchief and she lies, saying she could but won't produce it. Cassio finds the handkerchief in his room and, not knowing it is hers, gives it to his mistress, Bianca.

Act Four

Iago reminds Othello that Cassio has Desdemona's handkerchief. His psychological torture causes Othello to collapse in an epileptic fit. When he recovers he sees Iago talking to Cassio – they are talking about Cassio's mistress, Bianca, but Othello thinks they are talking about Desdemona. Bianca arrives holding the handkerchief. Othello recognises it as Desdemona's and vows to kill both her and Cassio. Lodovico arrives from Venice, with a letter recalling Othello and promoting Cassio to the command of Cyprus. Desdemona renews her pleas on Cassio's behalf, and Othello strikes her. Othello questions Emilia about Desdemona, but Emilia declares she is honest. When he questions Desdemona, she swears her innocence. Othello leaves and Desdemona asks Emilia to re-lay the wedding sheets on the marriage bed. Iago persuades Roderigo to ambush and kill Cassio. Othello sends Desdemona to bed, and she prepares sadly for sleep.

Act Five

The first scene is fast and furious. Roderigo cripples Cassio without killing him; Othello hears Cassio's screams and gloats that Desdemona's "dear lies dead"; Iago appears, pretending he has come to save Cassio, and kills Roderigo to silence him. He then declares that the murderer is Bianca. Othello joins Desdemona in her bedroom. She is asleep, but wakes when he kisses her. He questions her faithfulness, but she again declares her innocence. He smothers her. When Emilia calls from outside, Othello lets her in. Desdemona revives briefly, long enough to tell Emilia that she has killed herself, and dies. For a moment Othello shelters behind this deathbed lie, then confesses that he has murdered her. Emilia convinces him with remarkable ease that it was Iago who plotted against them both. Iago kills Emilia and flees. He is captured and, when he is brought back, Othello wounds him. Cassio tells Othello of Iago's villainy. Othello stabs himself and dies, kissing Desdemona.

What is *Othello* about?

For most of its history, *Othello* has been regarded as a play – or *the* play – about sexual jealousy and its devastating power. But it is about much more than that. In the play's first two acts we see Iago destroying the "grave and reverend" Senator Brabantio and the glamorously attractive Cassio, long before he goes to work on Othello in the play's second half.

In the figure of Iago, Shakespeare comes close to personifying outright malice – and the play shows how easy it is for someone malicious, ruthless and clever to manipulate others. In doing so, it offers us a disturbing view of human character as something changing and unstable: we are all more vulnerable to manipulation than we like to think, Shakespeare suggests, because our sense of "self" – of some Real or Inner Me – is a construct with scary faultlines. Things that we think of as unthinkable can be activated, and destroy our lives and those of others.

As Charles Nicholl shows in his book, *The Lodger*, Shakespeare was working on *Othello* in 1603, while living in an apartment in London's Silver Street. At the same time, he was working on another play with a sexual theme, *Measure for Measure*, and based both on Italian stories that he had found in the same book: Cinthio Giraldi's *Gli Hecatommithi* (1565) – or "A Hundred Tales". In both cases, however, he changed or keelhauled the original stories. Stephen Greenblatt once described the study of Shakespeare's sources as the elephants' graveyard of Shakespeare studies, and he has a point. Yet the changes Shakespeare made to these two Italian stories tell us a lot about what he wanted his very different plays to be about.

So, in the Italian story he turned into *Othello, The Moor of Venice*, the unnamed Moor and "Disdemona" have lived together happily for years, before the Moor is brought to suspect that his wife has been unfaithful. Shakespeare's lovers, on the other hand, have only just eloped and married when the play begins, and we learn in Act Two, Scene Three that they had not even had time to consummate their marriage before they set sail from Venice to Cyprus. Just why they had to make that journey in separate ships is not explained, but it is consistent with Shakespeare's drastic and, in the circumstances, cruelly purposeful compression of the Italian story's loosely indeterminate but extended time scheme: Shakespeare ensures that his couple have had almost no precious time together by themselves – even less than Romeo and Juliet. Although they love each other and are bravely committed to each other, they are denied any opportunity to know each other in those ways that require time and the prolonged intimacies of living together. This makes Othello's jealousy all the more startling, and gives the play its harrowing power.

Shakespeare makes other important changes to his source material. He turns Cassio, just a nameless officer in the Italian story, into Othello's closest, most loved friend and confidant, as well as the man he chooses to promote as his new lieutenant. The play thus revives one of Shakespeare's recurrent and even obsessive nightmares, the nightmare of double betrayal, in which a character thinks – rightly or wrongly, but usually wrongly – that the man he loves most has stolen the woman he loves most.

This nightmare had darkened the early comedy, *Two Gentlemen of Verona*, and was still churning in the very late comedy, *Two Noble Kinsmen*, which Shakespeare wrote with the successful newcomer, John Fletcher. It appears in *Twelfth Night,* when Duke Orsino thinks that "Cesario" (who is in fact a woman in disguise) has betrayed him with Olivia. And it triggers the tragedy in the first half of *The Winter's Tale*, when the suddenly demented Leontes becomes convinced that his oldest, closest friend, Polixenes, is his pregnant wife's lover. The recurring nightmare of double betrayal also generates the basic "story" in Shakespeare's *Sonnets*, where the middle-aged poet becomes ever more passionately involved with a beautiful, heartless young man who then, as the poet thinks, seduces the poet's

At a glance: how Shakespeare changed his source

CINTHIO'S *UN CAPITANO MORO*	SHAKESPEARE'S *OTHELLO*
Othello... unnamed, happily married for years	Othello... newly married
... a moor	... a Christian convert
... handsome; age not specified	... much older, more than 40
...hates the idea of leaving his wife behind	... doesn't mind if she stays in Venice
Cassio... married	Cassio... a Florentine bachelor
Iago, who has a daughter, is in love with Disdemona, but thinks she loves Cassio; he attempts to kill Cassio and beats her to death with a sand-filled stocking, while Othello stands by.	Iago childless
Othello tortured, incriminated by Iago, then banished, hunted down and killed by Disdemona's vengeful family	Othello kills himself; Brabantio dies of grief; after his arrest Iago, like Othello in Cinthio's tale, "never will speak"

mistress, the so-called "Dark Lady".

Othello is also a play that was, for its time, as savagely scathing about men's attitudes to sex, women and marriage as Ibsen's *A Doll's House*. The hero and Desdemona are the only couple to attempt any kind of enduring love relationship, but Shakespeare set them alongside two other couples – Cassio, the Florentine ladies' man pursued to Cyprus by the besotted Bianca, and Iago and his embittered, crypto-feminist wife Emilia. All three women are abused or exploited by their men, and the two wives are killed by their husbands.

In the last 20 years or so, however, the sense of *Othello* as a play about jealousy and betrayal has been overshadowed by a different argument. The question of race in *Othello* has come to dominate, both in recent criticism and in stage and screen productions. In her 1996 essay, "Shakespeare and cultural difference", the distinguished Indian critic Ania Loomba noted that of nearly 400 essays on *Othello* written in the previous five years, most had included some discussion of race. Had she analysed a similar sample a decade earlier, she wouldn't have found so many essays on *Othello*, and most would not have included a discussion of race.

The potent mixture of race and sex helps explain the play's current popularity. Edward Pechter is almost certainly right to say that Othello has become "the tragedy of choice for the present generation".

For many earlier generations, indeed for centuries, *Hamlet* had been the "tragedy of choice", not only in English-speaking countries but in 18th-century Germany, in early 19th-century Russia, and even in Japan, when Shakespeare finally arrived there with Chekhov, Ibsen and trams.*

This changed after the Second World War, when *King Lear* seemed to displace *Hamlet*. Many critics, notably R.A. Foakes in *Hamlet versus Lear*, were struck by this change and wanted to explain it. They related it to the sense of devastation caused by the war, to the influence of Jan Kott's *Shakespeare Our Contemporary*, to the "Theatre of the Absurd" and the plays of Beckett and Brecht, and to the changing practice of directors like Peter Brook, whose concern with bleakly contemporary drama fed back into their ways of directing Shakespeare. Brook's emphasis on the centrality of the actor in an "Empty Space" was also more suited to Shakespeare than traditions that derived from the 19th-century taste for spectacle – a taste that required geriatrically slow scene changes in lavish theatres.

In the devastated postwar period there was also a tendency to suppose that Shakespeare's most

---

* I once speculated with the critic A.D.Nuttall about what would have happened if Othello and Hamlet had been in each other's plays. The answer is that Othello would have killed Claudius immediately, sparing everyone a lot of grief. Hamlet, however, would have agonised endlessly about whether or not Desdemona was unfaithful and she would have probably ended up alive.

painful play must therefore be his most profound. Of course that does not necessarily follow; but in such a climate the American critic Stephen Booth's recent confession (in *Precious Nonsense*) that he thinks *Twelfth Night* Shakespeare's greatest play would have seemed astonishingly eccentric. It was only towards the close of the 20th century – as Michael Neill observes in his introduction to the new Oxford edition of the play – that *Othello* "began to displace" both *Hamlet* and *King Lear*: "critics and directors alike began to trace in the cultural, religious, and ethnic animosities of its Mediterranean setting, the genealogy of the racial conflicts that fractured their own societies".

So now, for many or most contemporary critics, *Othello* is above all about racism. There is no doubt that the racial angle plays on modern nerves, and race certainly features in the play: Iago is undoubtedly racist, as we discover very quickly. But to say that *Othello* is about racism is to kidnap the play. Shakespeare's principal preoccupations were different, as this book will try to show.

Does Othello love Desdemona?

In pondering the doomed love affair between Othello and Desdemona, critics have always disagreed about the character of Othello himself, and about the nature of the love between the ill-fated couple. How much does Othello really love the girl he eventually murders? Does he love her as much as she loves him?

In a ferocious but critically momentous 1937 essay, "Diabolic Intellect and the Noble Hero", the famous critic F.R. Leavis went so far as to deny that Othello ever loved Desdemona.

Leavis says little of what we see of the lovers in the play's first half, and bases his argument largely on Act Three, Scene Three, the so-called "Temptation Scene". During this, Iago talks to Othello about the "country disposition" of Venetian wives who

Let God see the pranks
They dare not show their husbands [3.3]

Othello has been a soldier and a mercenary for most of his life. He refers to his nine months or "moons" in Venice as his first extended experience of civilian life, and is not in a position to know much about the easy-going habits of Venetian wives. Having implied that Desdemona might be like them, Iago then recycles Brabantio's earlier warning to Othello. Brabantio says in Act One, Scene Three:

Look to her, Moor, if thou hast eyes to see:
She has deceived her father, and may thee. [1.3]

Now Iago reinforces this:

She did deceive her father, marrying you;
And when she seemed to shake and fear your
                                          looks,
She loved them most. [3.3]

And Othello's badly shaken response is, "And so she did."

This is evidence enough for Leavis, who pounces on Othello's apparent willingness to believe that his wife's impulsive decision to marry him could be a sign that she is fickle and untrustworthy. "There," Leavis sarcastically notes, "we have the noble and magnanimous Othello, romantic hero and married lover, accepting as evidence against his wife the fact that, at the willing sacrifice of everything else, she had made with him a marriage of romantic love. Iago points out that Othello didn't really know Desdemona, and Othello acquiesces in considering her as a type – a type outside his experience – the Venetian wife." Leavis then sweeps on to his no less angry verdict on Othello's "love": "It may be love, but it can only be in an oddly qualified sense love of her: it must be much more a matter of self-centred and self-regarding satisfactions – pride, sensual possessiveness, appetite, love of loving – than he suspects."

In Leavis's account, Othello and Desdemona

were never "romantic lovers" who could "live happily ever after". They were doomed from the start, and the destructive influence of "the demi-devil" Iago was almost superfluous. Othello, in Leavis's view, is destroyed by his own egotism. He is not capable of love. "Iago's power, in fact, in the Temptation Scene is that he represents something that is already in Othello: the essential traitor is within the gates."

Leavis's view is extreme and goes beyond what most people think the text suggests – which is that Othello does indeed love Desdemona. However, his passion for her is of a different nature to hers for him, and this has a critical bearing on what happens to them.

Early on, Shakespeare takes pains to emphasise what Ania Loomba calls the "enormous disparities of age, culture, and race" between the two, making very much more of these differences than the original Italian story did. The age difference figures along with Othello's "country" in Brabantio's frantic checklist of reasons why it was "Against all rules of nature" for his daughter – "in spite of nature,/Of years, of country, credit, everything" – to "fall in love with what she feared to look on".

The enormous racial and cultural disparity does not trouble the youthfully confident and brave Desdemona, when she says "I saw Othello's visage in his mind". Loomba and other critics have shown how, in Shakespeare's time, religion, not colour, was the main factor in promoting racial tension; but Shakespeare has, as it were, taken care of that by making his Moor a Christian convert who keeps referring to his "soul".*

How important is the age difference between Othello and Desdemona?

Shakespeare made his Moor very much older than Desdemona and considerably older than Iago, who actually tells us his age: he is 28, or "four times seven". We learn that Desdemona liked to talk and sing to her handkerchief, and we should probably think of her as being no older or not much older than Shakespeare's Juliet, who is 13, or Miranda in *The Tempest*, who is 14. In other words, if Iago is about twice Desdemona's age, Othello is three or four times her age.

We are often reminded of this age gap, as in Act Three, Scene Three when Othello has begun to fall apart and broods, "I am declined/Into the vale of years – yet that's not much..." Shakespeare seems anxious to show us that while Desdemona feels a youthful, physical passion, Othello's

---

* There is no textual evidence, incidentally, for the assumption made by Loomba and other critics that Othello must have been a Muslim before he became a Christian.

feelings are less straightforward.

In the original Italian story the Moor is delighted by his promotion to the Cyprus command but deeply grieved by the thought that he will have to leave his wife behind. "One day", when she sees him "so troubled" and "melancholy" she asks him why, and her passionately loving husband explains that "were I to leave you behind me, I should be hateful to myself, since in parting from you I should part from my own life".

Shakespeare changed all this. His Moor accepts without question, and with no evident disturbance,

SHAKESPEARE'S VENICE

The self-committing, idealistic Othello has committed himself three times over: first, to Desdemona, and, with some misgivings, to marriage; second, to a new faith, by becoming a Christian convert who refers to his "soul" more than any other Shakespearean character; third, to serving Venice, which now commands this once highly successful mercenary's complete and passionate loyalty.

Othello speaks of Venice with reverence, and says that serving it "makes ambition virtue". When Iago and Roderigo shatter his night in the first scene, Brabantio's initial response is incredulous: "This is Venice. My house is not a grange."

The Venice in *Othello* is very unlike the bustling, greedy Venice of *The Merchant of Venice*, or the corrupt city we find in Ben Jonson's *Volpone*.

Admired for its wealth, its cosmopolitan society and republican constitution, that Desdemona must be left behind in Venice. This is all the more striking because Shakespeare's lovers have only just married, and Othello must leave Venice before the marriage has even been consummated.

Nonetheless, Othello's immediate response to the news that he must leave within the hour is to boast a bit about his taste for "hardness" and to ask that his young bride be provided with Venetian "accommodation and besort" that "levels with her breeding". It then falls to Desdemona to tell the Duke, while apologising for her boldness or

which it fiercely defended against repeated Papal assaults and attempts to take control, this Venice, as Michael Neill puts it, was "the idealized city of classical theory – a place where the turbulence of individual emotion is subjected to the rational calm of authority".

Cyprus, on the other hand, which Shakespeare's audience knew as the Venetian colony briefly rescued from Turkish invasion by the celebrated Battle of Lepanto (1571), was an embattled military outpost – an island that "belongs to the stormy domain of the passions". Famous for its mythic association with the love-goddess, Aphrodite, Cyprus is linked within the play to the figure of Desdemona, who is subjected to a siege more dangerous than the Turkish assault on the island itself.

If Venice is a place of social order, Cyprus is suspended between this epitome of northern civilization and southern, barbarous/exotic Africa. This contrast reverberates through the play, as when Iago calls the marriage between Othello and Desdemona "a frail vow betwixt an erring barbarian and a supersubtle Venetian".

"downright violence", that she "did love the Moor to live with him", and that if she is "left behind" as a "moth of peace" she will be "bereft" of the "rites for which I love him".

Then, and only then, does Othello second her magnificent, youthfully romantic appeal, while insisting that in his case "appetite" for the "rites" of love that his young bride so longs for will never lead him to neglect his duties:

> *Vouch with me, heaven, I therefore beg it not*
> *To please the palate of my appetite,*
> *Nor to comply with heat, the young affects*
> *In my defunct, and proper satisfaction,*
> *But to be free and bounteous to her mind... [1.3]*

Othello's use of the word "defunct" has alarmed some editors and critics: in English it usually means "extinct" or "dead", but Othello is certainly not trying to reassure the Senators by telling them that he is impotent. Rather, with his emphatic negatives, "not" and "nor", and his disparaging references to the palate of appetite and sexual heat, he is insisting that he is no longer, if he ever was, swayed by "young affects", or youthful passions. Although such "young affects" had led Desdemona to deceive her father and elope with him, Othello goes on to scorn as "disports" and Cupid's "light-wing'd toys" those amorous rites which Desdemona desires so frankly, and with such chastely passionate eagerness:

> *And heaven defend your good souls that you*
> *think*
> *I will your serious and great business scant*
> *For she is with me. No, when light-winged*
> *toys*
> *Of feathered Cupid seel with wanton dullness*
> *My speculative and officed instrument,*
> *That my disports corrupt and taint my business,*
> *Let housewives make a skillet of my helm,*
> *And all indign and base adversities*
> *Make head against my estimation. [1.3]*

Shakespeare's Othello, unlike Cinthio Giraldi's passionate Moor, places great value on self-control. Significantly enough, he calls it "government": passions must be governed. He is not – to use Leavis's word – "romantic" in the way that Desdemona is. His very first words – when Iago tells him how some man (editors usually suggest Roderigo, but it could be Brabantio) "spoke such scurvy and provoking terms/Against your honour" and boasts that he thought to have "yerked" or knifed him, "here, under the ribs"– show his deep regard for civil law as well as self-government: "'Tis better as it is."

We hear him say similar things as the second scene unfolds. When Brabantio's posse arrives, Othello says, "Keep up your bright swords, for the dew will rust them," continuing:

> *Were it my cue to fight, I should have known it*
> *Without a prompter. [1.2]*

And Othello remains similarly controlled when
Brabantio sneers at his "sooty bosom".

We don't hear him having to fight for self-control
until the first night in Cyprus, when he has to quell
not only the public riot ("Are we turn'd Turks… For
Christian shame, put by this barbarous brawl") but
also his own inner turmoil, once he learns how
Cassio has betrayed his trust:

> *Now by heaven,*
> *My blood begins my safer guides to rule*
> *And passion, having my best judgment collied,*
> *Assays to lead the way. [2.3]*

We could put the contrast between the loyal
old soldier and the very young Desdemona this
way: the Senator's privileged young daughter trusts
her feelings in a supremely confident way. That
makes her the perfect victim for the perfect storm,
whereas her husband habitually reins in his
feelings, and only abandons himself, losing all
control, when he thinks that he has lost the woman
he loves.

When Othello and Desdemona are reunited
in the harbour scene, the difference in age – and

outlook – appears in yet another, deeply touching way. After greeting the "fair warrior" who had insisted on sailing to Cyprus and braved the terrible storm (while singing to her handkerchief), Othello tells his "soul's joy" that if this reunion were his last moment on earth it would be the happiest moment of his life:

> If it were now to die,
> 'Twere now to be most happy, for I fear
> My soul hath her content so absolute
> That not another comfort like to this
> Succeeds in unknown fate. [2.1]

Although this is wonderfully ardent, it might seem strange when the marriage has still not been consummated. The much younger, passionately loving Desdemona sees their reunion differently. She is thinking ahead when she replies:

> The heavens forbid
> But that our loves and comforts should increase
> Even as our days do grow. [2.1]

"Amen to that, sweet powers!" says Othello. He kisses her, and then acknowledges what has just happened in a surprisingly witty and gracefully loving way: he hopes that the difference this exchange reveals will be "the greatest discords" that "e'er our hearts shall make". In that moment, at least, he gets everything right.

Yet the difference this exchange reveals could – as Leavis, W.H. Auden and others have suggested – produce difficulties without the help of an Iago. Young Desdemona is naturally looking forward to the life that stretches out before her, whereas Othello, a much older, weathered warrior, no less naturally measures this new, ecstatic moment against his long, largely painful past. He thinks of his life as a pilgrimage that has finally and miraculously found its goal. But, as Desdemona tells him in Act Three, Scene Four, her young hand has "felt no age, nor known no sorrow".

That was, visibly, an awkward line for Maggie Smith to deliver in the 1960s Laurence Olivier *Othello*, since Smith was then 30. It seemed implausible that her mature Desdemona should say that she has known no age nor sorrow, even if we did not reflect that she is also forgetting about her heart-broken father (whom we later learn died of grief). Nor was it easy to imagine Smith's mature Desdemona talking and singing to her handkerchief on the voyage to Cyprus.

Two more examples from Act Three, Scene Four suggest how a mature actress playing the very young Desdemona will have one trouble after another. A few moments later, when Othello tells her of the handkerchief's magic powers, Desdemona's responses are girlish: "Is't possible?", "I'faith, is't

28

opposite: Maggie Smith as Desdemona in Stuart Burge's 1965 film

true?" Moments after that, when she so disastrously suggests that Othello's demand that she fetch the handkerchief is "a trick to put me from my suit" and asks, "Pray you, let Cassio be received again", Smith's mature Desdemona seemed irritatingly obtuse, because she was so evidently old enough to know better. Such troubles disappeared in Trevor Nunn's 1990 production (still available on DVD), when Imogen Stubbs played Desdemona as a young girl.

Nineteenth century critics usually gushed about Desdemona, but she tries the patience of some modern critics. In his famous essay, "The Joker in the Pack", W.H. Auden observed:

> Everybody must pity Desdemona, but I cannot bring myself to like her. Her determination to marry Othello – it was she who virtually did the proposing – seems the romantic crush of a silly schoolgirl rather than a mature affection: it is Othello's adventures, so unlike the civilian life she knows, which captivate her rather than Othello as a person.

Desdemona's love for Othello is more than a "romantic crush", but she *is* little more than a schoolgirl. Her youthful eagerness, indeed, seems less close to her husband's state of mind than to the generously vicarious pleasure with which Cassio anticipates the lovers' reunion and consummation:

> *Great Jove, Othello guard,*
> *And swell his sail with thine own powerful breath,*
> *That he may bless this bay with his tall ship,*
> *Make love's quick pants in Desdemona's arms,*
> *Give renewed fire to our extincted spirits* *[2.1]*

But then that frank and forward, happily human quality in Desdemona, to which fair young Cassio is so responsive, is something Othello seems both above and below. In Act One, Scene Three, he says he loved the "pity" with which Desdemona listened to his tales of intrepid adventures; and yet, as Tony Tanner has put it, he "seems to dread the sexual act". This difference between him and his bride may strike us as disquieting, in these early scenes. Later on it becomes momentously important, when these two idealists so lamentably fail to understand one other.

Why does Iago hate Othello so much?

If Desdemona loves Othello passionately, Iago hates him with an equal intensity, and it is Iago's hatred which drives the action of the play.

Iago is Shakespeare's most extraordinary example of a "surrogate dramatist" – that is, of a character within a play who makes almost everything that happens happen. In this respect, Iago's nearest rivals are Prince Hamlet in some parts of his play, Duke Vincentio in the second half of *Measure for Measure*, and Duke Prospero in almost all of *The Tempest*. But these other surrogate dramatists are also authoritative, privileged figures in their plays' respective worlds. They can and repeatedly do pull rank on those who are below them – whereas Iago is an army ensign who must rely on his wits to manipulate and destroy others.

It is not then surprising that Iago's part is huge, and larger than that of Othello. As R.A. Foakes observed, Iago has "32.58 per cent of the words in the play" and "43 per cent of the lines" in the first two acts. Act Two pretty well belongs to him. In 18th-century productions, Iago's part was often cut down; it seemed rather shocking that the play's villain had more to say than its tragic protagonist, and 18th-century critics found Iago rather vulgar – or far less fascinating than their 19th-century successors, who frequently wrote about the play as though it could or should have been called *Iago*. In dismissing the rumour that his new opera was to be called *Jago*, not *Otello*, Verdi commented that "it would seem hypocritical not to call it *Otello*" since he is the agent: Iago/Jago "is (it's true) the Demon who sets everything in motion, but Otello is the one who acts: He loves, is jealous, kills, and kills himself."

So why does Iago hate Othello so much? Coleridge famously wrote of his "motiveless malignity", calling it "fiendish" — as though Iago's urge to destroy is satanic or primeval, and doesn't have motives in any ordinary sense. Iago himself wouldn't have agreed with that, and many modern critics maintain that Iago's motives are clear enough. The play starts with his angry insistence that he hates the Moor. We then hear his long, angry account to Roderigo of how he was passed over for promotion, and we see how this intolerable wound to his self-esteem is festering. There is a racist element in his hatred, too: as soon as Brabantio appears, Iago abuses Othello as the "black Moor".

In considering Iago's fury at not being promoted, we should notice that his rank as the general's ensign or "ancient" is not as low as critics and directors often assume. He is a standard bearer, or "ensign". But he is no ordinary ensign, like Ancient Pistol in *Henry V*: as the general's personal standard-bearer he is third in command, so that his rank is much higher than that suggested in modern productions where he is a more insignificant and embittered NCO. In the third scene nobody raises an eyebrow when Othello entrusts "my wife" to "my ensign" in the dangerous voyage to Cyprus, and this is the first time that Othello refers to Iago as "honest": "A man he is of honesty and trust."

Of course, any failure to achieve promotion involves a nasty jolt or wound to self-esteem, which can usually be regarded as a mere product of the disappointment. But this play's first scene hints that Iago's furiously festering resentment may have a deeper cause than Iago himself can understand. Soon after his entry in the first scene he insists, "Not I for love and duty"; he is saying much the same thing (while referring to his rank) when he makes his hasty exit and explains that he "must show out a flag and sign of love,/Which is indeed but sign."

It is crucial to Iago and his self-regard – as it is crucial to Shakespeare's Falstaff, or to Thersites in *Troilus and Cressida*, or to the Bastard in *King John* and the bastard Edmund in *King Lear* – that he sees himself as a kind of truthteller, who knows and sees more than all the alleged superiors who outrank him. The truths that Iago thinks he knows are always reductive. His sense of himself and his "worth" or "price" is shaped – or fashioned, as Stephen Greenblatt would say – by his conviction that he is never taken in by pretty fictions and fabrications like "love" or "virtue" or "honour". For Iago, virtue is "a fig", "reputation" (or honour) is an "idle and most false imposition", and "love" is "merely a lust of the blood and a permission of the will".

Iago's use of the word "imposition" is interesting, because the word hadn't been used like that before. It suggests how, for Iago, virtue and honour and love are all constructs, or other people's foundational fictions – to use the terms that J.M. Coetzee uses in his 1997 collection of essays on censorship, *Giving Offense*:

> Affronts to the innocence of our children or to the dignity of our persons are attacks not upon our essential being but upon constructs – constructs by which we live, but constructs nevertheless. This is not to say that affronts to innocence or dignity are not real affronts... the infringements are real; what is infringed, however, is not our essence, but a foundational fiction to which we more or less wholeheartedly subscribe, a fiction that may well be indispensable for a just society, namely, that human beings have a dignity that sets them apart from animals and consequently protects them from being treated like animals.

Part of Coetzee's point is that, even when we see what they are, we cannot abandon all such "constructs" and "foundational fictions" without surrendering human dignity and responsibility. But, for Iago, seeing through and rejecting all such "impositions" is what puts him several steps ahead – so why is he behind, when the play begins, and Cassio has been "preferred"?

That question is already eating Iago alive when he insists "Not I for love and duty", and when he determines to produce his own brutal black comedy to show how vile and stupid creatures like Cassio and Othello really are. The first scene is enough to show that Iago doesn't lack motives. If anything, he has too many, like people whose feelings are too easily hurt because they have too many feelings. When Coleridge referred to the "motive-hunting of motiveless malignity", he was commenting on Iago's soliloquy at the end of Act One, when Iago suddenly comes up with yet another motive for hating Othello so much:

> *I hate the Moor,*
> *And it is thought abroad that 'twixt my sheets*
> *He has done my office. I know not if 't be true,*
> *But I, for mere suspicion in that kind*
> *Will do as if for surety.* [1.3]

Could Othello have slept with Emilia? Most critics don't take this new motive seriously, and we can't tell how seriously Iago takes it. As Robert Heilman pointed out, his use of the word "and" is startling: "rarely is a conjunction used so effectively: the hate is prior, and a motive is then discovered."

Edward Pechter extends Heilman's shrewd point when he writes: "Iago's motivations are fabricated after the fact out of little or nothing; even the real ones seem inadequate to explain the intensity of his malice." So it looks as though Coleridge was on to something after all, like Auden when he called his famous essay on Iago "The Joker in the Pack". Iago is driven by his need to bring everything down.

The great German critic A.W. Schlegel was noticing this when he shrewdly commented on the relation between Iago's cleverness and ignorance:

> Accessible only to selfish emotions, he is thoroughly skilled in rousing the passions of others, and availing himself of every opening which they give him: he is as excellent an observer of men as anyone can be who is unacquainted with higher motives of action from his own experience.

What is so impressive about this sentence is that it explains how the conditions of Iago's appalling power are also weaknesses: Iago is, after all, sometimes wrong. For example, his belief that Desdemona's love for Othello is perverse lust is wildly wrong – but he goes on believing it. Nor does he ever suspect that his own wife will betray him – by exposing his villainy – and sacrifice her own life to "love and duty".

Iago's declared opposition to "love and duty" makes more sense later in Act One, when we see how the idealistic, self-committing Othello lives for these ideas, or foundational fictions. He has committed himself not only to his love for Desdemona, but to Christianity, and to serving the republican state of Venice which "makes ambition virtue" (See "Shakespeare's Venice" p.22). When

the play begins the idealistic Othello has triumphed on all three fronts: as Iago says to Cassio in the second scene, he's "made for ever". The contrast between the two men is clear: the reductive truthtelling on which Iago's self-regard is based has brought him nowhere, whereas Othello's idealism, and idealistic view of himself, has brought him everything. This is agony to the Iago who later observes that Cassio "hath a beauty in his daily life that makes me ugly".

Should this startling remark be attributed to envy, or jealousy, or both? The distinction between jealousy and envy seemed clear enough to Arrigo Boito, who wrote the libretto for Verdi's *Otello* – and also wrote: "Othello is Jealousy and Iago Envy." If challenged, Boito might well have explained that Othello is jealous, but never envious, whereas Iago is constantly envious, perhaps adding that envy is always low or demeaning.

Whether Iago's jealousy is sexually driven is another question. Orson Welles insisted that Iago must be impotent. Freud maintained that delusional jealousy always includes a homosexual component, and many actors and directors have believed that Iago's hatred of Othello stems from suppressed feelings of lust. Whether or not this is true, it is clear that Iago's hatred goes beyond mere hatred of being passed over and indeed beyond all ordinary or familiar motives – which is what Coleridge was suggesting.

opposite: Ian McKellen as Iago with Imogen Stubbs as Desdemona, 1990

This does not mean we have to go as far as the 19th-century critics who regarded Iago as a devil incarnate, or as an abstract personification of "Evil" with a capital "E". As the critic G.K. Hunter says in his superb *History of English Drama 1586-1642*, Iago is no "stage devil": "his motivations belong clearly enough to a recognisable human type" who finds "power and pleasure in seeing others suffer, especially those believed to be superior or even invulnerable".

How is Iago so successful?

As the philosopher Ludwig Wittgenstein once remarked, Sigmund Freud's method of argument involved persuasion, not evidence: his patients and readers were persuaded that what they didn't want to know, or thought unthinkable, was likely to be what they needed to know – or rather, believe. Iago must persuade his victims to believe what cannot be proved, because it is not true, and his tactic or method could be compared with that of the author of *The Interpretation of Dreams* (1900) and inventor of the "Oedipal complex". Indeed, the first great success of Iago's own "Freudian" method comes in the first scene, when after being told Othello is in bed with Desdemona, Brabantio, her father, suddenly feels driven to admit:

This accident is not unlike my dream,
Belief of it oppresses me already. [1.1]

When Brabantio says this he has not been confronted with, let alone convinced by, anything that could be called evidence. He does not even do what Roderigo suggests, and check to see whether Desdemona is still at home or in her "chamber". Instead, the terrible bombardment of obscenities about what "the Moor" is doing to his daughter "now, now, even now" unhinges the "grave and reverend" Senator's judgment by triggering some "dream" or nightmare that he had hitherto suppressed when he "oft invited" Othello to his home. Brabantio has been persuaded by what is, to use his own significant phrase, "palpable to thinking", and then perceives things differently.

In Act Two's harbour scene Iago goes to work again, this time on Roderigo. Roderigo is already Iago's victim or "gull" when the play begins: Iago has been fleecing him by promising to deliver Roderigo's various gifts to Desdemona and then keeping them for himself. Now Iago goes a step further.

In the harbour scene, Desdemona is anxious because her husband still has not arrived. The gallant Cassio tries to calm her and Iago and Roderigo observe him kissing her and paddling his fingers in her palm. Iago knows perfectly well that Cassio is not Desdemona's lover; so does Roderigo, and so do we. But Iago can see how what he and Roderigo have just seen could submit to that different interpretation, which he immediately tries out on Roderigo. It is an illustration of one of the key themes of the play: that seeing is not knowing.

Roderigo immediately, and rightly, dismisses Iago's interpretation. But Iago is not deterred. He doesn't seek to present any evidence.* He simply tries to undermine Roderigo's confidence in his own ability to read the signs. (He will do this again in Act Three, Scene Three when he persuades Othello to think that the Venetian woman he loves is like the other Venetian wives of whom Othello knows nothing.) And like Brabantio, Roderigo quickly collapses and agrees that Cassio and Desdemona could be lovers. Just as Brabantio speaks of what is "palpable to thinking", Iago speaks no less hauntingly of what is "probal to thinking".

Iago's next victim, later in the second act, is Cassio. His first challenge is getting Cassio drunk, which isn't difficult. Cassio can't hold his drink; as he himself says, he has "very poor and unhappy

---

* *Othello* is full of legal language. The play stands the idea of justice on its head, but the lexicon of justice pervades it (as it does *Measure for Measure*, written in the same year). As Tony Tanner has put it: "arraignment and accusation; defence and pleading; testimony, evidence, and proof (crucial word); causes, vows, oaths; solicitors, imputations and depositions – the law is, somehow, everywhere in the air".

brains for drink". Othello presumably knows of this "infirmity" when he gently warns Cassio not to "out-sport discretion", but Cassio has already ignored that warning and had "but one cup" – just one! – before Iago goes to work on him.

Iago faces a far more testing challenge when Cassio is devastated by shame at what he has done. Here it's worth noticing another significant departure from the Italian story, where the Cassio figure's offence is far less grave – "un picciolo fallo", or small fault, as Desdemona says when pleading with the Moor. Shakespeare made Cassio's offence far more grave, so that it is jolting to hear Desdemona describe it as a small matter that scarcely deserves a private rebuke: "not almost a fault/T'incur a private check".

On this, the first occasion when Othello trusts his closest friend and new lieutenant to take his place (the literal meaning of lieu-tenant), Cassio gets drunk, attacks Roderigo with his sword, severely wounds the much admired ex-governor of Cyprus, and starts a riot in a city under martial law.* Cassio is getting off lightly when he is just dismissed. He has every reason to be devastated by shame, and no good reason

* As Thomas Styward warned in his military conduct book *The Pathway to Martial Discipline* (1581), no soldier – let alone a lieutenant – "shall be suffered to be of ruffian-like behaviour" or "injure any of his fellow soldiers with any weapon, whereby mutinies often ensueth, upon pain of the loss of his life".

SIX KEY QUOTES

66 *Your daughter and the Moor are now*
Making the beast with two backs 99 [1.1]

66 *O curse of marriage,*
That we can call these delicate creatures ours,
And not their appetites! 99 [3.3]

66 *Virtue! A fig! 'tis in ourselves that we are thus or*
thus. Our bodies are gardens, to which
Our wills are gardeners 99 [1.3]

66 *If it were now to die,*
'Twere now to be most happy, for I fear
My soul hath her content so absolute
That not another comfort like this
Succeeds in unknown fate 99 [2.1]

66 *O, beware, my lord, of jealousy!*
It is the green-eyed monster which doth mock
The meat it feeds on 99 [3.3]

66 *then, must you speak*
Of one that lov'd not wisely but too well;
Of one not easily jealous, but, being wrought,
Perplex'd in the extreme; of one whose hand,
Like the base Indian, threw a pearl away
Richer than all his tribe 99 [5.2]

to excuse what he has done.

But he can be of no use to Iago unless he can be persuaded to ask Desdemona to negotiate on his behalf, and thus Othello's suspicion can be roused. So Iago, always quick to spot weakness, plays on Cassio's self-love. He persuades Cassio that although his capacity for self-criticism is one of his most attractive features he is "too severe a moraler", and owes it to himself to see that his actions were not his actions but the result of the "devil" in drink. Seeing how readily Cassio responds to these invitations to be lenient on himself is theatrically riveting and morally dreadful.

Iago's destruction of Cassio in Act Two, Scene Three is like the final dress rehearsal before he finally goes to work on Othello in Act Three, Scene Three, the play's central scene and one of the greatest scenes in world drama. This scene, like the whole second act, belongs to Iago.

Iago is successful because of his extraordinary resourcefulness in taking opportunities when they're offered and turning even unpromising circumstances to his advantage. He is helped, however, not just by luck (as when Desdemona's handkerchief comes into his possession), but by the way all the major characters play into his hands.

Is Othello too easily jealous?

In the play's final scene, Othello describes himself as "one not easily jealous, but, being wrought,/ Perplex'd in the extreme". Critics have always argued about this: isn't it wildly implausible that, despite Iago's cunning, he could possibly believe his wife had betrayed him within a few days of marrying her?

Leavis's answer to this, as we have seen, is that Othello loves himself, not Desdemona, and is quite willing to believe what is patently untrue: Iago is "subordinate and merely ancillary", a "necessary part of the dramatic mechanism".

Before Leavis, the prevailing view was the one shared by the early twentieth century Shakespearean critic A.C. Bradley and the Romantic poet Samuel Coleridge: that Othello is a "Noble Moor" whose claim to be "not easily jealous" is justified; he has been driven out of his wits by the demon-like cunning of Iago. (Interestingly, as John Bayley once wryly observed, Bradley's view of Othello coincides with Othello's view of himself, whereas Leavis's view of Othello as a deluded egotist corresponds with Iago's view of Othello.)

The Bradley/Coleridge view is more plausible than Leavis's. It does have a major flaw, however: neither of these critics seems to have realised how close they come to arguing that murdering Desdemona would have been all right, or compatible with Othello's awesome nobility, if only she *had* committed adultery. On the other hand, they are surely right that it required what Bradley called Iago's "diabolic intellect" to bring Othello down.

"Let me repeat," Coleridge wrote in a famous passage:

> Othello does not kill Desdemona in jealousy, but in a conviction forced upon him by the almost superhuman art of Iago, such a conviction as any man would and must have entertained who had believed Iago's honesty as Othello did.

Iago is certainly skilful but his task is made much easier by the way Cassio and Desdemona behave.

After Cassio has been dismissed and before he urges Desdemona to plead for his reinstatement, Emilia, Iago's wife, reassures him in Act Three, Scene One that "all will sure be well":

> *The general and his wife are talking of it,*
> *And she speaks for you stoutly; The Moor replies*
> *That he you hurt is of great fame in Cyprus*
> *And great affinity;*
> *And that in wholesome wisdom he might not but*
> *Refuse you; But he protests he loves you*
> *And needs no other suitor but his likings*
> *To take the safest occasion by the front*
> *To bring you in again. [3.1]*

This is an important speech. Cassio's offence is a grave betrayal of Othello's loving trust and in his irresponsible behaviour he has shown other aspects of his character that make it easier to see why Iago loathes him – and hard to agree with Bradley, who talks of the "moral beauty" of his character.

After joining in the soldiers' song about King Stephen, Cassio declares, in his drunkenness, that although the song is "exquisite", he will not hear it again because "I hold him to be unworthy of his place that does these things". The suddenly pompous ass then adds that "there be souls must be saved, and there be souls must not be saved". The ever vigilant Iago replies, "It's true, good

THE THEORY OF DOUBLE TIME

The time scheme of Othello has perplexed many critics. There is a gap between Acts One and Two to allow for the voyage to Cyprus, but after that the action takes place in just two days, or rather two nights. (Fittingly, most of the action of the play occurs at night; Iago works best in the dark.) But how can so much happen in such a short time? When Iago suggests to Othello that Desdemona is tired of him, how can that be – after just two days? Othello speaks of Cassio and Desdemona's "stolen hours of lust": when were they? Bianca accuses Cassio of neglecting her a week, but Cassio has only been in Cyprus a day. And Othello cries: "Iago knows/ That she with Cassio hath the lieutenant" – playing to this sudden revelation of Cassio's concern with his "place" in the next world as well as this one.

Cassio continues: "For mine own part – no offence to the general, nor any man of quality – I hope to be saved." When Iago replies, stroking the same soft spot, "And so do I too, lieutenant", Cassio declares, "Ay; but by your leave, not before me. The lieutenant is to be saved before the ancient."

This brief exchange reveals a side to Cassio that we haven't seen or expected before. His pride in his new rank, his maudlin religiosity and his snobbish reference to "men of quality", which clearly excludes the man he is talking to, come across as grubbily

act of shame/A thousand times committed." When?

The ingenious theory of "double time" was developed in 1849-50 by "Christopher North" (Wordsworth's friend John Wilson) to explain the discrepancies: the main action is set over just two days because that is what makes the play so dramatically effective, but at the same time Shakespeare makes us think the time is actually longer – long enough for adultery to be possible.

As the critic John Dover Wilson later claimed, in proudly bardolatrous fashion, Shakespeare's use of double time allowed him to solve a "difficulty" which "might well have seemed insuperable to any ordinary dramatist", for "if Othello and Desdemona consummated their marriage during the first night in Cyprus, when could she have committed the adultery Iago charges her with"?

The play answers that question in Act Three, Scene

unattractive. We begin to wonder why Othello thought him worthy of the office he holds.

Indeed when, afterwards, his punishment is merely to lose his office, he is getting off lightly. Yet despite this he continues to behave recklessly. Emilia tells him that Othello is prepared to forgive and reinstate him. He "needs no other suitor" but Othello himself: all he must do is wait. If Cassio were a more intelligently loyal friend, he would at once abandon his (or Iago's) plan of involving Desdemona. Instead, he ignores what Emilia says and persists in appealing to Desdemona.

Three, when we learn, with Iago, that Cassio had not only accompanied Othello when he was wooing Desdemona but had "many times" been alone with her in the months of courtship. The perverse alternative answer provided by the "double time" theory produces a far worse "difficulty": where on earth is Othello sleeping during his greatly extended stay in Cyprus? And wouldn't he notice Desdemona's absence?

In fact, most of the instances which trouble critics have an explanation which doesn't require any tortuous theory. The "stolen hours" of lust between Cassio and Desdemona were clearly supposed to have happened before the marriage. Bianca evidently followed Cassio to Cyprus from Venice, thus making her remark about not seeing him for a week quite logical. The only real problem is the quick revocation of Othello's commission: a new governor, Lodovico, arrives to replace him only a day after Othello himself has arrived. But even here, it might be supposed that Brabantio's faction in Venice plotted to have Othello overthrown and replaced the moment the latter had left to take up his post.

This is not just unnecessary but unwise, as is Desdemona's own behaviour when she agrees to press his case – having already shown her youth-fulness in her naively uncomprehending insistence that Cassio's "trespass" was trifling. In her girlish way, she is flattered, even flustered, by Cassio's appeal. She then forgets or ignores her husband's wholly justified point that "wholesome wisdom" made him dismiss Cassio and that he can't reinstate his lieutenant until a little time has elapsed.

As Auden puts it:

> A sensible wife would have told Cassio this and left matters alone. In continuing to badger Othello, she betrays a desire to prove to herself and to Cassio that she can make her husband do as she pleases.

Othello's promise to reinstate Cassio because he "loves" him reveals the Moor as a man ready to trust his own generous impulses: this decision may be imprudent but it is noble, and provides another example of finely calibrated characterisation. We see here both the experienced general and the man whose "free and open nature" appeals to the naive and impulsive Desdemona.

So, before Iago begins his assault in Act Three, Scene Three, Othello is badly let down and jolted by the behaviour of the girl, as well as the man, he loves and trusts most. Emilia's report makes

Desdemona's appeal redundant, even offensive. She may be brave and generous, but she is very green and acts thoughtlessly.

If we are not yet wondering whether she knows herself well enough to have chosen a husband wisely, we will be by the end of the play, when we hear her murderer trying to exonerate himself by claiming to be what she so much more obviously is, or was: "one that loved not wisely, but too well".

At this point, though, her foolish behaviour, and Cassio's, makes Iago's task all the easier because it leads Othello to think they are behaving suspiciously. What makes it easier still is that by this point Othello and Desdemona have almost certainly not made love, so Othello can't be sure – once Iago begins to turn the screw – whether his wife is a virgin or not.

So is Othello's marriage ever consummated?

The text of the play suggests that the answer to this question is no.

At the beginning of Act Two, Scene Three we learn that Othello and Desdemona have not consummated their marriage when they arrive in Cyprus: Othello tells Cassio to take charge and report to him early the next morning, then says to Desdemona:

Come, my dear love,
The purchase made, the fruits are to ensue:
That profit's yet to come 'tween me and you. [2.3]

In the play's first scene Iago had told the horrified Brabantio that "now, now, very now, an old black ram/Is tupping your white ewe", and later added: "your daughter and the Moor are now making the beast with two backs." But, as we learn in Act Two, Scene Three, that was not happening, since the lovers were – and go on being – interrupted. Now, finally, they do go to bed.

This first night in Cyprus is their first chance to consummate their marriage. Indeed Iago tells Cassio nastily that "our general" must not be blamed for neglecting his duties by rushing off to make love to Desdemona – which of course smears Othello by suggesting that he *is* neglecting his duties:

Our general cast us thus early for the love of his
Desdemona – whom let us not therefore blame;
he hath not yet made wanton the night with her,
and she is sport for Jove. [2.3]

But thanks to Iago, the lovers will be interrupted on this first night in Cyprus. And this is their one and only opportunity, since Othello murders Desdemona on the second night.

This, incidentally, raised a different question that obsessed some 19th-century critics: how could Desdemona ever find the time – or, why could Othello not see that Desdemona never had time, even if she had the inclination – to make love with Cassio? The answer to this is that they had plenty of time – before their marriage. It is only if we use the word "adultery" in a strict, legalistic sense that we have problems seeing when it might happen. But what warrant does the play provide for supposing that Othello is concerned only with what might have happened after his marriage? The answer is none.

Before the marriage, Desdemona had plenty of opportunity to be unfaithful. Shakespeare takes pains to let us know that Cassio acted as an intermediary in the courtship between Othello and his bride-to-be and they were thus alone together "many times", not in Cyprus but in Venice.

And Iago's insinuation, in Act Three, Scene Three, is that something took place before the wedding, something that can be expected to continue and that would explain Desdemona's passionate concern to have Cassio reinstated.

As to what happens between Othello and Desdemona that first night in Cyprus, before Iago engineers the riot – it is a matter of interpretation. After quelling the riot, Othello goes off to dress Montano's wounds, while Desdemona goes back to bed. The question of how much time they have alone together before, and after, they are disturbed is greatly complicated by the extraordinary way in which the whole night passes during the scene. When Act Two, Scene Three begins the lovers go off to bed; when the scene ends dawn is breaking.

But whether or not Othello and Desdemona had time to consummate their marriage in the night, the evidence of the play suggests they did not.

Firstly, in Act Four, Scene Two, Desdemona instructs Emilia to "lay", or re-lay, "on my bed my wedding sheets"; in the next scene when Emilia duly reports that "I have laid those sheets you bade me on the bed", Desdemona gives Emilia a still more pathetic and premonitory instruction. "If I do die before thee, prithee shroud me/In one of those same sheets." Presumably Desdemona would not ask Emilia to relay, and would not ask to be shrouded in, a bloodied wedding sheet.

Secondly, in Act Five, Scene One, when Othello hears Cassio's screams and thinks he has been murdered, the "Noble Moor" – who has instructed Iago to murder Cassio but maintains in the final scene that he is "An honourable murderer, if you will/For nought I did in hate, but all in honour" – gloatingly says:

'Tis he. O brave Iago, honest and just,
Thou hast such noble sense of thy friend's wrong!
Thou teachest me. Minion, your dear lies dead,
And your unblest fate hies; strumpet, I come.
Forth of my heart those charms, thine eyes, are
blotted;

Thy bed, lust-stained, shall with lust's blood be spotted. [5.1]

The last line is clearly spoken by a man who would notice, and even look for, bloodied sheets, if he had "taken" Desdemona's virginity on that first night in Cyprus.

There is another more obvious reason to doubt the marriage's consummation. If Othello shed Desdemona's blood by taking her virginity on the first night in Cyprus – as he would do except in the unlikely event that her hymen had been accidentally ruptured beforehand – he would surely notice he had done so and thus know she was a virgin and could not have made love with Cassio once, let alone "a thousand times". Only a mental defective could first take his wife's virginity and then, the morning after, become convinced of her continued infidelity. Moreover, by drastically shortening the time scheme of the original Italian story, by contriving to keep his newly married lovers apart, and by drawing attention to the wedding sheets in both Act Four and Act Five – and earlier, ironically, to Desdemona's strawberry-spotted handkerchief – Shakespeare clearly intended us to think about this.

To put it another way, if the marriage had been consummated, it would be hard to see how Othello could be tricked by Iago.

There is no conclusive proof that Desdemona

is still a virgin when she dies, but all the evidence suggests it. The final scene, which Dr Johnson famously described as unendurable, becomes more unendurable than ever if we suspect that the murder is this marriage's only consummation, and the ghastly tragicomic parody of an erotic "death". This would also provide the most terrible and poignant explanation of Othello's strange comment when he is convinced of Desdemona's innocence and holds the body that is now dead and cold:

> Cold, cold, my girl?
> Even like thy chastity. [5.2]

What view of character emerges from *Othello*?

In *Othello*, as in *Measure for Measure*, the play he wrote in the same year, Shakespeare is terrifyingly concerned with what we have it in us to become.

Although critics like Bradley and Leavis have very different views on what motivates Othello, they both see him as behaving "in character" throughout and this character, in their view, is "set". For Leavis, murdering Desdemona is consistent with what he refers to as Othello's "essential make-up". For Bradley, as for Coleridge,

Othello is always noble, so his bad behaviour must be attributed to external influence. The influential American critic, Stephen Greenblatt, takes yet another view of Othello's character, but one that also emphasises its consistency. In Greenblatt's judgment – one of the oddest made about this play – he behaves as he does because he is driven by Christian guilt: he believes that his own love for Desdemona is akin to adultery and kills her and himself as a result (see below).

What these judgments have in common is that they take a static view of the self as some

OTHELLO THE GUILTY CHRISTIAN

Iago's "dark enterprise" is to convince Othello not that Desdemona has been unfaithful but that he, Othello – the newly converted Christian – has committed an unpardonable sin by enjoying sex with his own wife. This is the theory developed by the distinguished American critic, Stephen Greenblatt.

Greenblatt believes that "the religious sexual doctrine" in which Othello believes is at first concealed in the play but eventually "becomes increasingly visible". Like many "New Historicist" arguments – "New Historicism" being the movement which holds that Shakespeare's works can only be understood in the context of the history of the period (i.e. as museum pieces) – this is curious since what becomes "increasingly visible" had remained invisible for four centuries, and certainly wasn't visible to earlier, Christian critics like Dr Johnson and Coleridge.

Greenblatt's analysis of

kind of fixed core or essence – the Real Self or Inner Me. The play, on the other hand, implies a more fluid, dynamic view of the self as a kind of matrix or ensemble of different possible selves that include all that we have in us to become.

In his fascinating study, *Othello and Interpretive Traditions*, Edward Pechter notes that "it is only when a man's 'character' is pictured as a sort of hard, fixed core somewhere inside him... that looking for 'flaws' in it makes any sense". Pechter then observes how "modernist critics from Leavis onward, despite their anti-Bradleyan

---

Othello in *Renaissance Self-Fashioning* (1980) is brilliantly original. But it is based on a very partial sampling of the text. It is also built on a very partial sampling of the critics – so partial that while he mentions a few Americans, he completely ignores Coleridge, Bradley and every other English critic

Greenblatt's understanding of Christianity, too, is very selective. He concentrates on those early Christian Fathers who took up St Paul's exaltation of celibacy ("It is better for a man not to touch a woman", etc) with an anti-sexual vengeance

that dominated orthodox doctrine from the fourth to the 14th centuries.

So Greenblatt gives special emphasis to St. Jerome's re-workings of the stoic Xystus's maxim that "He who loves his own wife too ardently is an adulterer", and to the 16th-century Protestant theologian John Calvin's warning that "the man who shows no modesty or comeliness in conjugal intercourse is committing adultery with his wife". After quoting another priest, Nicholas of Ausimo, who says that the "conjugal act" is only without sin "if in the performance of this act there pronouncements, are in practice as locked as critics from Bradley backward into an idea of character as a stable, autonomous and coherent entity". To borrow the writer William Hazlitt's apt phrase, the critics whom Pechter questions are all wanting to "perceive a fixed essence".

Othello's character, however, comes over not as fixed but as unstable. Consider his judgments of Cassio, which lurch from one extreme to the other, like his later judgments of Desdemona. Having dismissed his lieutenant for drunken behaviour, he

is no enjoyment of pleasure", Greenblatt concludes that virtually all relevant Christian edicts are "in agreement that the active pursuit of pleasure in sexuality is damnable".

To put it mildly, this is a highly coloured version of Christian doctrine. Greenblatt never mentions St Thomas Aquinas or Peter Lombard, for example, neither of whom takes nearly such an extreme view, nor does he mention that Calvin, despite his warning, actually repudiates Jerome's argument that "if it is good not to touch a woman, it is bad to touch one": on the contrary, Calvin argued,

sexual intercourse is a pure institution of God, and the idea that "we are polluted by intercourse with our wives" emanates from Satan, not Paul. In these cases the writers are emphasising the need to respect one's wife, not the damnability of taking pleasure in marital intercourse.

Nor does Greenblatt ever discuss or even mention Martin Luther, who strongly defended Christian marriage, arguing that a nun's celibacy does not confer a higher spiritual state than that of a faithful Christian wife, or Erasmus's wonderful colloquies on marriage, which clearly influenced later tells Desdemona that he "loves" him, and will reinstate him on a "safer occasion". By the end of Act Three, Scene Three, however, Othello is ordering Iago to kill Cassio, and in Act Four, Scene One he is wanting to throw Cassio's nose to a dog and wishing that he himself could spend "nine years a–killing" him and so on, until the horrible moment when Othello hears Cassio screaming, and gloats that Desdemona's "minion lies dead".

His vile lines at this point drip with hatred for Desdemona as well as Cassio, but within a few

---

Shakespeare in his creation of the witty, un-neurotic, sexually frank women of his romantic comedies.

Even more ridiculously, Greenblatt's only textual authority for this extra-ordinary claim is Iago's soliloquy at the end of Act One, when Iago is trying to work out what to do, and suddenly thinks: "I have it!" Here are the relevant lines from Iago's soliloquy.

Cassio's a proper man: let me see now,
To get his place, and to plume up my will
In double knavery. How? How? Let's see:
After some time to abuse

Othello's ear
That he is too familiar with his wife. [1.3]

Pronouns in English can be maddeningly ambiguous, but in this case the lines that are most urgently relevant to Iago's plan could be glossed as follows:

After some time, to abuse Othello's ears,
That he [Cassio] is too familiar with his [Othello's] wife:

In Greenblatt's reading, the crucial line has to be glossed very differently: "He [Othello] is too familiar [ie impassioned, meaning minutes, and perhaps even more horribly, the demented Othello will be maintaining that he did nothing "in hate, but all in honour". This is so manifestly untrue as to be preposterous; but Othello is desperately struggling to rescue and preserve his sense of himself as truly "noble" – "one that loved not wisely, but too well", "one not easily jealous", an "honourable murderer, if you will". He can only do that by denying that his actions were his actions, and attributing them to the "demi-devil" Iago, who "ensnared" his "soul and body".

---

adulterous] with his [own] wife."

In other words, Othello has been so carried away in his lovemaking that he has treated Desdemona like a whore; being "too familiar" with his wife then deeply troubles him (though never, it seems, her) because he is a recent Christian convert, and "cannot allow himself the moderately flexible adherence that most ordinary men have toward their formal beliefs". We are to suppose that somehow, and rather miraculously, Iago senses or divines these dirty secrets in a soliloquy he speaks before the first night in Cyprus – that is,

before Othello has had any opportunity to make love to his wife at all, let alone be "too familiar" by turning the "rites" that Desdemona eagerly anticipates into something unspeakably awful. The "dark essence of Iago's whole enterprise" will then be "to play upon Othello's buried perception of his own sexual relations with Desdemona as adulterous".

It is nonsense, of course, even if we believe that the marriage between Othello and Desdemona is consummated. If it isn't, which the text suggests is the case, Greenblatt's reading falls apart anyway.

Something similar happens to Cassio on the first night in Cyprus, when he betrays Othello and himself. At first Cassio sees his actions as his actions, and is overwhelmed by shame at what he has done. He tells Iago: "I have lost my reputation. I have lost the immortal part of myself, and what remains is bestial." This thought becomes more general (moving from "I" to "we") when he moans about how "we transform ourselves into beasts!" He then exclaims: "To be now a sensible man, by and by a fool, and presently a beast – O strange!"

We have already seen such a transformation take place in Brabantio, when the "grave and reverend" Senator Brabantio turns into a racist babbling of witchcraft; we see it taking place in Cassio in this scene, and we will then see how the "Noble Moor" is even more horribly transformed. But when Cassio says these things, he is already wanting to attribute his own actions to the "devil drunkenness", just as we will see Othello wanting to attribute his actions to the "demi-devil" Iago. Both men want to regard the "devil" as external to their tenderly nursed sense of some blameless Real Self or Inner Me.

From a modern perspective, one of the most extraordinary aspects of this play is the way in which it persistently exposes and opposes its own characters, and their own alarmingly confident use of metaphors that imply some static, rather

TEN FACTS
ABOUT OTHELLO

1.

Iago is the third longest part in Shakespeare's plays.
Of *Othello*'s 3323 lines, Iago speaks 1098, almost
250 more than Othello himself – only Richard III,
at 1171, and Hamlet, at 1476, have more.

2.

Othello is one of four Shakespearian Moors. The
others are the Prince of Morocco and a nameless
Moorish girl made pregnant by Launcelot Gobbo
in *The Merchant of Venice*, and Aaron in *Titus
Andronicus*.

3.

The critic Stanley Cavell is among those who
have pointed out the "satanic cores" in the names
of Othello and Desdemona – "hell" and "demon" –
though less simple etymologies have been
suggested. The name Desdemona, from Cinthio's
Un Capitano Moro, may come from the Greek
κακότυχοσ, meaning ill-fated.

4.

Desdemona's willow song is only included in the folio edition (Act Four, Scene Three):

> The poor soul sat sighing by a sycamore tree,
>   Sing all a green willow;
> Her hand on her bosom, her head on her knee,
>   Sing willow, willow, willow:
> The fresh streams ran by her, and murmur'd
>   Her moans;
> Her salt tears fell from her, and soften'd the
>   Stones...
> Sing all a green willow must be my garland.
>   Let nobody blame him, his scorn I approve...
> I call'd my love false love; but what said he then?
>   Sing willow, willow, willow:
> If I court moe women, you'll couch with moe men,

The earliest known setting of these words to music dates from 1583; the song has subsequently been set to music by Erich Korngold, Sir Hubert Parry, Arthur Sullivan and Ralph Vaughan Williams.

5.

Othello forms the basis of two operas. Rossini's *Otello* is based only loosely on the play, premiered in Naples in 1816. Verdi's *Otello* – his penultimate opera – was filmed in 1986 by Franco Zeffirelli, and starred Plácido Domingo.

6.

Paintings inspired by *Othello* include Eugène Delacroix's *Othello and Desdemona* and *Tragedy of Desdemona* (1847-1849) and Dante Gabriel Rossetti's *Desdemona's Death Song* (1878-1881). Other artists to have painted scenes from *Othello* include Théodore Chassériau, Alexandre-Marie Colin and Frederic Leighton.

7.

At least eight films have been made of *Othello*, the first in 1909, when silent films were made in both Italy and Germany. The extreme financial troubles that beset Orson Welles' 1952 version are recounted in Micheál MacLiammóir's *Put Money in Thy Purse*. The most recent, directed by Oliver Parker, starred Kenneth Branagh and Laurence Fishburne, the first black actor to play Othello on screen.

Both the BBC and ITV have attempted *Othello*: Jonathan Miller's 1981 adaptation cast a blacked up Anthony Hopkins as Othello, to public outcry. A 2001 ITV drama made Othello the first black Commissioner of the Metropolitan Police.

8.

Samuel Pepys refers to *Othello* three times. In October 1660 at the Cockpit, on which occasion "a very pretty lady that sat by me, called out, to see Desdemona smothered". In 1666, reading *Othello* "which I ever heretofore esteemed a mighty good play" he deemed it a "mean thing"; he thought *A Midsummer Night's Dream* "insipid and ridiculous" and *Romeo and Juliet* "a play of itself the worst that ever I heard in my life". He also saw *Othello* in 1669 at the King's Playhouse, when Desdemona was played by Margaret Hughes, probably the first professional female actress to appear on the English stage.

9.

Othello is one of two of Shakespeare's plays set in Venice (though only the first act), the other being *The Merchant of Venice*. Curiously, not one of his 37 canonical plays is set in Elizabethan or Jacobean England. They are all set abroad or in ancient Britain (*King Lear*, *Cymbeline*) or in medieval and early Tudor England (the histories).

10.

The biographer Peter Ackroyd, however, sees *Othello* as reflecting contemporary English worries about blackamoors. In 1596, Elizabeth I issued an edict against "the great number of negars and blackamoors which are crept into the realm since the troubles between Her Highness and the King of Spain", saying "there are already here too manie". (A large colony of Moors existed in London, mostly refugees from Spanish persecution.) Ackroyd sees other Spanish parallels: Philip II was reputed to have been insanely jealous, and to have strangled his wife in her bed; "what is more, he had become suspicious of her when she had inadvertently dropped her handkerchief".

than dynamic, concept of the Self. They talk of seeing what cannot be seen or known. Lodovico is astonished when his original perception of Othello turns out to be mistaken: "Is this the noble Moor, whom our full Senate/Call all in all sufficient?" Desdemona's affirmation that she saw Othello's "visage in his mind" tells us more about her mind than Othello's: she certainly did not see the mind of her murderer. Like many critics, the play's characters themselves think of the inner self as a kind of fixed core which is predictable and visible, unlike the play's dynamic conception of the self as a family of possible selves, or a matrix of all that we have it in us to become.

Iago, alone, understands the way in which people deceive themselves and that the seeds of his victims' destruction lies within them. When Othello asks him, in Act Three, Scene Three, to reveal his "worst of thoughts" he protests,

> *Why, say they are vile and false?*
> *As where's that palace whereinto foul things*
> *Sometimes intrude not? who has a breast so pure*
> *But some uncleanly apprehensions*
> *Keep leets and law-days, and in sessions sit*
> *With meditations lawful? [3.3]*

Iago demonstrates how Brabantio, or Cassio, or

Othello, with his "free and open nature", can all be transformed into "beasts". When Cassio speaks of how one can be "now a sensible man, by and by a fool, and presently a beast", he is already wanting to excuse or disown what his actions and speech had revealed about himself — like someone who says "I'm sorry, I wasn't myself", without wanting to think about whatever is implied by that curious split between the Subject "I" and the Self, or two selves, in question.

Under Iago's influence, Othello begins to imagine and say things that are unquestionably foul or filthy. In the first of his jealous soliloquies in Act Three, Scene Three, he says:

> *I had rather be a toad*
> *And live upon the vapour of a dungeon*
> *Than keep a corner in the thing I love*
> *For others' uses. [3.3]*

When, later in the scene, he says he could have gone on being happy so long as he didn't know that Desdemona had betrayed him, he doesn't just say, "I had been happy if I had nothing known." He puts that thought in an atrociously dirty-minded way:

> *I had been happy if the general camp,*
> *Pioneers and all, had tasted her sweet body,*
> *So, I had nothing known. [3.3]*

The idea of the whole army gang-banging Desdemona is revolting, of course. Othello's idea of Desdemona's "sweet body" as something – some *thing* – to be "tasted" is also appalling, but shameful in a different way. "Pioneers and all" is especially foul, because pioneers were the lowest type of soldier and were responsible for heavy duty tasks like digging roads and trenches – or digging mines and countermines. Othello is not only thinking of Desdemona's "sweet body" as a thing to be "tasted" or relished by some sexual gourmet, he is also thinking of it as something to be mined. Even the final word of Othello's sentence, "known", has a sexual as well as a cognitive sense: in Biblical English the sons of God "know" the daughters of men when they possess them sexually. So does the word "occupation" when he says his "occupation's gone". The word "occupy" had a sexual sense or meaning long before Shakespeare wrote *Othello.*

The striking thing about Othello's jealousy, as Michael Neill points out, is "the intensely erotic charge" it gives to his language. As he imagines the possibility of Desdemona's betrayal, he seems to long for the very thing he dreads: "be sure thou prove my love a whore... give me the ocular proof... Make me to see't... Would I were satisfied." It is as if he wants to turn his own wife into a whore, and in this scene and Act Four, Scene Two, the so-called "Brothel Scene" (where he treats Emilia as a brothel-keeper), the "real secret laid bare", says Neill, is "Othello's own repressed desire":

> This is not to say that the Moor wishes to prostitute his wife in any literal sense – only that it is through the jealous fantasy of her body becoming an object of satisfaction for other men that he first discovers the terrible depth of his own need for her.

As a result he is trapped in what the critic Harry Berger calls a sado-masochistic "sinner's discourse", a condition that drives him to enlist Iago's aid as "the scourge or justicer who will help him procure the sinner's keen and bitter pleasure of hurting, punishing, destroying himself by hurting, punishing, destroying what, next to himself, he most loves".

This can happen, Berger suggests, because the one thing Othello fears more than Desdemona's faithlessness is her faithfulness – the extravagant abandon of a desire that invites equal self-abandonment from him.

Othello's collapse is all the more striking because of the pride he took in his iron self-control: his very sense of himself depended on a capacity for self-mastery so absolute that it rendered him immune to extremes of passion. The irony of his plight is that the "Chaos" he imagines as the consequence of ceasing to love Desdemona comes upon him precisely because of his submission to that love.

The psychic disintegration he experiences, in a play which calls into question the very concept of "character", shows strongly in his language in the last two acts, as in the confused speech before his epileptic fit at the beginning of Act Four:

> *Lie with her? Lie on her? We say lie on her when they belie her! Lie with her, zounds, that's fulsome! Handkerchief! confessions! Handkerchief!... It is not words that shakes me thus. Pish! Noses, ears, and lips! Is't possible? Confess? handkerchief! O devil!* [4.1]

It is hard to believe this is the same man we saw and heard in the first act; having prided himself on his self-discipline and restraint, he has gone so completely to pieces as to seem almost unrecognisable.

In what light does the play show us male attitudes to women?

In its exploration of male attitudes to women and marriage, the play invites us to see parallels between Othello and Desdemona and the two couples set alongside them. All three men, Othello, Cassio and Iago, are instinctively distrustful of marriage.

Othello, for example, tells Iago in Act One, Scene Two that there is something he must "know", or understand:

> *But that I love the gentle Desdemona,*
> *I would not my unhoused free condition*
> *Put into circumscription and confine*
> *For the sea's worth. [1.2]*

Othello's fear of domesticity and of marriage as confinement is more easily understood when we learn that his whole life has been spent in the field, and that his "nine moons" or months in Venice were his first experience of civilian life. A. D. Nuttall once described Othello as a hero who steps into a house.

But his fear is shared by the much younger Cassio. In the first scene of the play, Iago describes him as "A fellow almost damned in a fair wife" – for Iago, to be almost married is to be almost damned. The woman he is referring to is Bianca, Cassio's mistress, whom he has so far resisted marrying. Bianca's name, translated into English, means "white", which is a rather grim joke if, like some critics, we trust Iago when he describes Bianca in Act Four, Scene One, as a "hussy" who:

> *by selling her desires*
> *Buys herself bread and clothes: it is a creature*
> *That dotes on Cassio – as 'tis the strumpet's*
> *plague*
> *To beguile many, and be beguiled by one. [4.1]*

In both the First Folio and the Quarto, the word that is used to describe Bianca's occupation is not "hussy" but "Huswife", which could mean a hussy or even prostitute, but could also mean a housewife or householder. And if we read or listen to Iago with any closeness, which we should be doing long before Act Four, we can smell a rat even here. He says that her situation in "doting" on Cassio is like that of strumpets or prostitutes, whose "plague" it is to dote on one man while having to sleep with many. Bianca certainly dotes on Cassio, and she may be his kept woman; but there is no evidence or sign that she has other lovers, or customers.

The misfortune that ruins her life is that the glamorous but puddle-deep Cassio wants nothing more than a convenient sexual liaison.

Iago knows this, and uses it at the beginning of Act Four to deceive Othello. He pretends to Othello that he is going to question Cassio about Desdemona – and tells Othello to hide and listen. In fact, his plan is to talk to Cassio about Bianca, and he anticipates Othello's reaction:

As he shall smile, Othello shall go mad.
And his unbookish jealousy must construe
Poor Cassio's smiles, gestures, and light
                                    behaviour
Quite in the wrong. [4.1]

Iago then gets Cassio going by saying "I never
knew a woman love man so", and by reminding
Cassio that Bianca "gives it out that you shall
marry her". It is clear that Iago knows a great deal
about the relationship, as he would do since it has
clearly been going on in Venice before the play
opens.

Now Bianca has followed Cassio to Cyprus,
and Cassio tells Iago about her determined pursuit
of him:

CASSIO:
> *She was here even now; she haunts me in*
> *every place. I was the other day talking on the*
> *sea-bank with certain Venetians, and thither*
> *comes the bauble and, by this hand, falls thus*
> *about my neck –*

OTHELLO:
> *Crying 'O dear Cassio!' as it were: his gesture*
> *imports it.*

CASSIO:
> *So hangs and lolls and weeps upon me, so*
> *shakes, and pulls me! Ha, ha, ha! [4.1]*

As Iago predicts, this scene drives Othello mad as he completely misunderstands it. But the scene also shows that Cassio clearly lacks the "moral beauty" which the critic A.C. Bradley saw in him. He is selfish and ruthless in his exploitation of Bianca: his contemptuous word "bauble" reflects on himself rather than on her, since that is all Bianca is to him – a plaything. She loves him and wants to marry him, but he wants nothing more than a sexual liaison (in ironic contrast to Othello, who seems to want the love but not the sex).

As for Iago, he is an out-and-out misogynist and his wife, Emilia, is one of Shakespeare's most original creations. Nineteenth-century critics tended to dislike her, but nowadays there is some danger of sentimentalising Emilia as a crypto-feminist, although her fierce dislike of men and her husband's misogyny are two sides of the same marital coin. In the play's final scene we may well feel torn in two directions when Emilia shows such (fatal) courage in denouncing her husband but also reviles Othello as a black devil through and through. This breach in our own responses follows from our earlier, divided response when Emilia, who so obviously suffers as a neglected or abused wife, nonetheless betrays Desdemona by stealing for her husband the handkerchief he so badly wants, while asking "What will you give me now?"

However mixed our reactions to Emilia, there is no doubting the force of the famous speech in which she fiercely denounces male double standards.

> *But I do think it is their husbands' faults*
> *If wives do fall.....*
> *   Let husbands know*
> *Their wives have sense like them: they see and*
> *   smell,*
> *And have their palates both for sweet and sour*
> *As husbands have. What is it that they do*
> *When they change us for others? Is it sport?*
> *I think it is. And doth affection breed it?*
> *I think it doth. Is't frailty that thus errs?*
> *It is so too. And have not we affections,*
> *Desires for sport, and frailty, as men have?*
> *Then, let them use us well: else let them know,*
> *The ills we do, their ills instruct us so. [4.3]*

Shakespeare doesn't align himself and his play with Emilia to nearly the same extent that Ibsen aligns himself with Nora in *A Doll's House*. Emilia's generalised view of men and their appetites is no less prejudiced than her husband's misogynistic attitude to women (which is echoed by Othello's "O curse of marriage/That we can call these delicate creatures ours/And not their appetites!") In this respect Iago and Emilia are very much a couple: their views of the other sex are complementary; they are the twin products of a loveless and barren marriage.

Nor does Shakespeare encourage us to take an uncritical view of Desdemona. W.H. Auden, who, as we have noted, didn't like her, pointed to the way she talks to Emilia in Act Four, Scene Three. After expressing her admiration for Lodovico she turns to the topic of adultery:

> Of course, she discusses this in general terms and is shocked by Emilia's attitude, but she does discuss the subject and she does listen to what Emilia has to say about husbands and wives. It is as if she had suddenly realised that she had made a *mésalliance* and that the sort of man she ought to have married was someone of her own class and colour like Lodovico. Given a few more years of Othello and of Emilia's influence and she might well, one feels, have taken a lover.

We may resist Brabantio's view in Act One that his own daughter is externally fair but subtly duplicitous. Yet she has successfully deceived her father through all the months of a secret wooing when Othello and Cassio were clandestine visitors. Brabantio is a tragically betrayed father, and his uncaring or unimaginative daughter can apparently forget her father's agony and humiliation when she tells Othello that the hand he is holding, "that gave away my heart", also "hath felt no age, nor known no sorrow". We learn in Act Five that her father has died of a broken heart; nor would

Shakespeare have included that information in a busy final act unless he wanted spectators to think about it. He makes sure, as Auden says, that we don't forget the effect she's had on her father. In effect, Desdemona kills him, just as Othello kills her.

This, of course, does not justify Othello's murder; nor are we meant to think it does. For all the ambiguities, the play offers a more damning view of male attitudes than many of Shakespeare's works. Desdemona, Bianca and Emilia suffer terribly at the hands of their men, all of whom, in their different ways, are insensitive to the needs of their women. As Ania Loomba observes in *Shakespeare, Race and Colonialism*: "There are only three women in *Othello* — Bianca, who is treated as a whore, Desdemona, who is repeatedly accused of being one, and Emilia, who is dismissed as her 'bawd'." The two married women are in the end both killed by their husbands.

Why is Othello's "Had it pleas'd Heaven" speech so important?

The key speech in Othello's collapse – perhaps in the play itself – comes in Act Four, Scene Two, when he is interrogating Desdemona about her fidelity (see the next page for the First Folio version).

Many modern critics don't see this speech as important; neither Leavis nor Greenblatt even refer to it. But in the 19th century it was seen as crucial. The great Italian actor Tommaso Salvini, whose legendary performances as Othello rocked Europe and England (despite the fact that he played the part in Italian), saw it as the most important in the play. As Salvini himself put it, "Had it pleas'd Heaven" showed how Othello's love is "the pure affection of a soul which unites itself to another, and without which he could no longer exist".

Othello's syntax is remarkably controlled when the speech begins and it remains so for as long as he is considering what agonies he could bear ("Had it pleas'd heaven to try me", etc). But once he begins to consider reality, and the idea that he has been "discarded", an extraordinary meltdown follows. The agony of confronting what cannot be endured produces a breakdown that is terrifyingly complete because it is syntactic and logical, as well as emotional and psychological. No other English poetic dramatist depicts breakdown in this comprehensive fashion. The speech then plunges into the chaos and incoherence of its final lines.

The impression of coherence in the first half of the speech owes a lot to the astonishing sequence

> Had it pleas'd Heaven,
> To try me with Affliction, had they rain'd
> All kinds of Sores, and Shames on my bare-
> head:
> Steep'd me in povertie to the very lippes,
> Given to Captivitie, me, and my utmost hopes,
> I should have found in some place of my Soule
> A drop of patience. But alas, to make me
> A fixed Figure for the time of Scorne,
> To point his slow, and moving finger at.
> Yet could I beare that too, well, very well:
> But there where I have garnered up my heart,
> Where either I must live, or beare no life,
> The Fountaine from the which my current
> runnes,
> Or else dries up: to be discarded thence,
> Or keepe it as a Cesterne, for foule Toades
> To knot and gender in. Turne thy complexion
> there:
> Patience, thou young and Rose-lip'd Cherubin
> Ay, there, look grim as hell!

The series
of liquid
metaphors

As speech begins to break
down, Shakespeare combines
the liquid metaphor with
the different idea of storing
or garnering

Now comes the climactic and obscene
metaphor, with its image of the current
of Othello's life drying up and turning
into a cistern (or water-tank) in which
foul toads (or other men) can knot and
gender (or make babies)

of liquid metaphors. This sequence begins when
Othello imagines God raining down "sores and
shames" on his "bare head", like that of Job in the
Bible. It continues with the idea of being steeped
in poverty "to the very lips". Still, Othello insists,
he could have found in his "soul" some drop of
"patience". The liquid metaphors reach a climax
with the idea of Desdemona as the fountain
from which his own current flows – so that he
"cannot exist", as Salvini put it, if he is
"discarded thence".

At this point – the point which precipitates
the meltdown moment – the climactic fountain
metaphor is suddenly combined with the very
different idea of garnering, or storing. The classically-
minded Dr Johnson objected to this mixed
metaphor, but it is very precise in what it tells us
about the nature of Othello's love – and, arguably,
about love in general, and all acts of valuing. When
we love or value someone or something, we want to
believe that we are recognising, not creating or
constructing, the value. The garnering part of the
mixed metaphor suggests how the idealistic Othello
has in one sense given – endowed or invested –
Desdemona with the unique value she has for him:
he has garnered up his heart by making her his
storehouse of value.

But then Othello has detached this value from
his own act of valuing, as the fountain part of the
"mixed" metaphor suggests: having given Desdemona

her significance or value for him, he now believes it exists as something objective, quite separate to him. She is now the "fountain" or source from which his own life derives significance or value.

As Othello contemplates this his manner of talking changes, with terrifyingly suddenness, as though a switch has been thrown – and yet the whole speech has been moving, purposefully, towards the moment when he confronts what cannot be endured. His syntax, and use of metaphor, is superbly controlled while he is considering what he could have endured in situations which he imagines. But then, when the meltdown moment finally arrives, the series of liquid metaphors produces another climactic but obscene metaphor: the fountain from which the "current" of his own life flows, or "dries up", turns into the cistern (or water-tank) in which other men or "foul toads" can "knot and gender" (or make babies).

The cistern metaphor perverts both parts of the earlier mixed metaphor: both Othello's idea of garnering up his heart by endowing Desdemona with unique value, and his sense that the value and meaning of his own life then flows from her fountain. The image shows Othello's mind flooding with horror, as he imagines his wife letting in other men. For the first time in this speech, he sounds like Leontes in *The Winter's Tale*, who imagines,

Цветной художественный
фильм

ОТЕЛЛО

(По трагедии В. Шекспира)

Сценарий и постановка   СЕРГЕЙ ЮТКЕВИЧ
Главный оператор   Е. АНДРИКАНИС
Композитор   А. ХАЧАТУРЯН

В роли Отелло—СЕРГЕЙ БОНДАРЧУК

crazily, how his own wife's "belly" will "let in and out the enemy" with its "bag and baggage" (testicles and seed). There is a hint of something similarly crude earlier in *Othello*, in Act Three, Scene Three, when the Moor talks of the "corner" of Desdemona that he "keeps", at his own expense, for other men to "use".

But now Othello starts to sound just like Leontes. Leontes's whole speech is the demented raving of a man suffering from delusional jealousy, a jealousy which, in this case, is self-generated, without the help of an Iago. Leontes has suddenly become insanely convinced that his faithful, pregnant wife Hermione has betrayed him with his oldest, most dearly loved male friend, and he talks, wildly, of having a neighbour "fish" in "his pond" and of other husbands who "have gates" that their wives' lovers open. Othello comes to use similar language, but the first half of his speech is not crazy, which is what makes it all the more shocking.

His purpose in "Had it pleas'd Heaven" is to divorce what he takes to be his "real" self from what he takes to be his "real" situation. He clings to and insists on the reality of his noble Self by imagining situations which that Self could some-how endure and survive, while also insisting that this "real" Self can "bear no life" in what he wrongly takes to be his "real" situation. In effect, the speech is announcing the death of the only Self this Subject will acknowledge, while insisting that Desdemona killed it.

This is tragic in one way: the ascent to the fountain metaphor measures the great difference between the idealistic Othello and the deranged Leontes, although the cistern metaphor then shows Othello plunging down to Leontes's level. What he is trying to do is absolve himself, in advance of the murder he commits, by blaming Desdemona for killing the Real Me. His "noble" and "patient" Self is then supplanted by some Other Self, which he refuses to acknowledge as his own – even though this supplanting Self is no less "real", and will murder Desdemona.

How important is Othello's colour?

For a long time after the first performance of Othello, race was scarcely an issue for critics. It wasn't until the early 19th century, as Edward Pechter observes, that "interpreters" in Britain and America "invented colour as a central topic of the play".

Several Romantic writers started worrying about the degree of Othello's blackness, with Coleridge the crucial figure. The passage most frequently quoted occurs in *Table Talk*, where Coleridge's nephew Henry Nelson Coleridge recorded his uncle's insistence, in a conversation in April 1823, that Desdemona could never have fallen in love with a blackamoor or "veritable negro":

> As we are constituted, and most surely as an
> English audience was disposed in the beginning
> of the 17th century, it would be something
> monstrous to conceive this beautiful Venetian
> girl falling in love with a veritable negro. It would
> argue a dispro-portionateness, a want of balance
> in Desdemona, which Shakespeare does not appear
> in the least to intend.

On another occasion, the nephew reported
Coleridge's insistence that "Othello must not be
conceived as a negro" and that "There is no ferocity
in Othello; his mind is majestic and composed."
Although Coleridge thought it would have
been "monstrous" for Shakespeare to have
"conceived" Othello as a "veritable negro", Bradley
says that that is precisely how Shakespeare did
conceive him – as black, not tawny. Bradley (in
1904) also says something remarkably daring:

> I will not discuss the further question whether,
> granted that to Shakespeare Othello was a black, he
> should be represented as a black in our theatres now.
> I dare say not. We do not like the real Shakespeare.
> We like to have his language pruned and his
> conceptions flattened into something that suits our
> mouths and minds. And even if we were prepared to
> make an effort, still, as [Charles] Lamb observes, to

imagine is one thing and to see is another.

The narrator of Julian Barnes's novel *Flaubert's Parrot* remarks on "what a curious vanity it is of the present to expect the past to suck up to it". Bradley is making the same point and he is right to do so. Othello, after all, talks of his own blackness when he describes his face as "begrimed and black" and later wonders whether Desdemona might have

BLACKING UP

The first white actor to "black up" playing Othello was Richard Burbage, Shakespeare's contemporary and leading man and the first Othello in 1604, just as he was Shakespeare's first Hamlet, Macbeth and Prospero. The tradition of blacking up didn't trouble the play's early audiences and continued more or less unchallenged until 1814, when the great Romantic actor Edmund Kean chose to play Othello as a tawny Moor; many later 19th-century actors followed suit and sometimes wore flowing Oriental robes – like the renowned Tommaso Salvini, who so deeply impressed Verdi and Henry James.

Kean decided to play a tawny Moor at the very time when arguments about the degree of Othello's blackness were beginning. Nonetheless, if we can trust his biographers, Kean appears to have decided to make the Moor tawny not black so that his facial expressions would be more visible in the outsize theatres of the time, not because he was anticipating Coleridge's notorious view that Desdemona could never have fallen in love with a blackamoor or "veritable negro".

discarded him because "I am black" and "declined/ Into the vale of years – yet that's not much".

Othello's blackness is clearly important to the story. We don't see him until the second scene. Before that, everything that we hear about his appearance – the "textual evidence" – is a stream of filth flowing from the mouths of Iago and Roderigo, who hate Othello and find his blackness disgusting. Iago tells Desdemona's horrified father that

In the 20th century blacking up has proved highly contentious. Ian McKellen, one of the great modern Iagos, said he would never play Othello:

> Every modern white actor, taking on Othello, feels obliged to explain why he's not playing him black, which was surely Shakespeare's intention, when the unspoken reason is that to "black up" is as disgusting as a "nigger minstrel show".

In 1964, Laurence Olivier blacked up to play perhaps the most controversial modern Othello. The production, directed by John Dexter, owed much to Leavis's conception of the Moor as a deluded egotist and Olivier, to quote Michael Neill, played him as a "vain and posturing barbarian whose thin veneer of civilisation disintegrates under pressure". Olivier's own conception of the part, according to Kenneth Tynan, was of "a Negro sophisticated enough to conform to the white myth about Negroes, pretending to be simple and not above rolling his eyes, but in fact concealing (like any other aristocrat) a highly developed sense of racial superiority". For Tynan this portrait of "a triumphant black despot, aflame with unadmitted self-regard", was entirely persuasive. Others were less sure, and in the years that followed

Even now, now, very now, an old black ram
Is tupping your white ewe [1.1]

This encourages us, as well as Brabantio, to imagine the "tupping" (a nasty word used of mating animals) and even the bed that we will finally see in the last scene: we are being caught up in something dirty-minded. Iago then associates Othello's blackness with that of the traditional Christian

---

many Othellos reverted to variations of the orientalized Moor of the Victorians. But this didn't please everyone either. When Paul Scofield chose (in *The Times's* phrase) "the light dusky tan of a desert ruler", Ian Stewart in *Country Life* complained that the sexual and racial tensions of Olivier's performance had disappeared, as had the heroic soldier's terrifying "collapse into primitive" chaos". Nor was Sheridan Morley, writing in *Punch*, satisfied with Donald Sinden's over-civilised Arab:

> Othello does not need to become the black-and-black minstrel that Olivier made of him, only a chorus line away from the Swanee River. He

does, however, have to be capable of falling for Iago's duplicity.

Morley's implication that the part would be best left to black actors proved prophetic: for the next couple of decades, more and more Othellos were black. But this created problems of a different kind.

Paul Robeson's famous Othello in 1930 had been praised because, in the words of one reviewer, of his convincing "relapse to a barbaric rage" and by implication because of the "childishness, temperament and innate barbarism" he shared with Shakespeare's character. Robeson didn't mind this, seeing the play devil by telling Brabantio that "the devil will make a grandsire of you". Worse follows with Iago's terrible warning that "you'll have your daughter covered with a Barbary horse, you'll have your nephews neigh to you, you'll have coursers for cousins and jennets for germans" – since "your daughter and the Moor are now making the beast with two backs". Again there is the ferocious stress on what is happening now: imagine, imagine! Poor Brabantio is imagining

as a mirror for "the position of the coloured man in America today". But in the different climate of the 1980s and 1990s, black actors were less sanguine. As Neill has put it: "even as aesthetic and political pressures converged to make the casting of white actors to the lead role appear increasingly undesirable, black actors themselves were repeatedly disabled by fear of the racial stereotyping that might ensue from a full commitment to the emotional excess and extravagant theatricality of the part."

The impasse made Othello harder than ever to cast, with many black actors refusing to play the part because they feared fuelling or reviving racist stereotypes by "going bananas" in front of largely white audiences. The superb Shakespearean actor Patrick Stewart agreed in 1997 to play Othello in a New York production – but he stipulated that his Othello would be white and the rest of the cast would be black.

This attitude, and others like it, incensed some Shakespeare lovers. Geoffrey Wheatcroft, in *The Sunday Telegraph*, blamed modern sensitivities on an over-reaction to Laurence Olivier's Othello, and urged white actors to challenge "the odious notion [of black-only] casting by demanding to play the part – blacked-up or *au naturel* as the theatre pleases"; if refused, he said, they should sue under the Race Relations Act.

it, and this unhinges his mind. The "grave and reverend" senator, and "much belov'd" magnifico, turns into a bigot who babbles of witchcraft.

It is therefore a shock in the second scene when we first see Othello, and see him remaining majestically composed when Brabantio insultingly refers to his "sooty bosom". What we later see of Othello suggests that we should dismiss Iago's dirty-minded reference to the "Moor" as a sexually ferocious "ram" or "Barbary" stallion as abusive chaff, while allowing the accuracy of the two other items: Othello's blackness is not in doubt, and he is also "old" – or older than Iago. But he is noble and dignified and not the man we have heard described.

The shock we receive here is significant because this is a play in which we are constantly being made aware of the difference between seeing and imagining. (The critic James Hirsh has aptly called it "a tragedy of perception".) Once we see Othello for ourselves, we can doubt or reject what Iago and Roderigo see. But the play clearly intends us to be disturbed by seeing the old, black and probably ugly Moor – he is the Moor of Venice and he should stand out – with the senator's young white daughter.

In this important sense the play's first scene is doing to us what Iago does to his victims. In Act Three, Scene Three, when Iago finally goes to work on Othello, he at first refuses to say what he suspects. The maddened Othello protests that Iago has "shut up" in his own mind some "Monster" or "horrible conceit" that is "Too hideous to be shown". But then, when Othello struggles to make out in his own mind what the "Monster" is, he creates it, which is of course what Iago has been engineering. Once Othello has admitted the "Monster" into his own mind by giving it imaginative house-room, he has made it his own. It is more difficult to expel or expunge.

This is akin to the situation of the audience in the first scene. We hear monstrous accounts of Othello, and when we finally see him, we must weigh what we have heard, and may have been tempted to imagine, against what we actually see.

Blackness is important in *Othello* in another way. Like the *Sonnets*, the play is full of images and metaphors based on the idea that white is good and black is bad. The metaphorical association between the black and the foul or dirty is not only deeply rooted in our own culture, as in others, but also preceded any direct cultural contact with black peoples. It stems, presumably, from cleaning what is sooty or begrimed, and is no more racist than the way that the Japanese as well as the British and Americans speak of bank accounts "going into the red" without intending any smear on North American Indians or Russians. So we understand what Othello means when he says that Desdemona's "name" is "now begrimed and black/As mine own face" by realising that this is an anguished, violent variation on the metaphorical idea of blackening someone's name. And when Desdemona says that she saw Othello's "visage in his mind", she means that, for her, his external blackness counts for less than his internal qualities and virtues.

The Duke praises Othello's virtues in similar terms to Desdemona's father, Brabantio, when he says:

> *If virtue no delighted beauty lack,*
> *Your son-in-law is far more fair than black. [1.3]*

Brabantio's shocking response to this is to suggest that his fair daughter is in fact foully deceptive ("far more black than fair") and having deceived him may deceive Othello too.

Can *Othello* be seen as a racist play?

The colour question in the play has worried many critics and led to interpretations which place a heavy emphasis on it. In the 19th century, *Othello* was often seen as a portrait of a primitive man living in a sophisticated society who lapses back into barbarism.

The first to make this argument, and to connect Othello's jealousy to his race was the famous

German critic August Wilhelm von Schlegel, who translated 17 of Shakespeare's 37 plays into his native language.* To suggest a connection between race and jealousy was less dangerous then than it is now, and Schlegel fearlessly rushed in, where angels, and the more politically correct, feared to tread. He argued, in his Vienna lectures, that Othello's "savage" component was peculiar to Othello and those "burning climes" which have "given birth to the disgraceful confinement of women and many other unnatural uses". In Schlegel's view, Othello's colour disposed him to an extreme, ultimately murderous form of sexual jealousy that does not afflict white men; his was not the jealousy of the heart which is compatible with the tenderest feeling and adoration of the beloved object.

It is true that in his popular history of Africa, the Moorish writer Leo Africanus seems almost proud of what he describes as his own people's inclination to murderous sexual jealousy, and Shakespeare would certainly have read John Pory's 1600 translation of Africanus's book. Moreover, Africanus's folk belief makes a brief appearance in the Italian story that was Shakespeare's primary source, when Disdemona tells her husband that "You Moors are

* Extraordinarily, Schlegel translated Shakespeare's verse into verse and his prose into prose. Just as extraordinary, he also translated Dante, Calderón, Cervantes and Camoens, and edited Ramayana and the Bhagavad-Gita.

so hot by nature that any little thing moves you to anger and revenge".

Few prominent critics have been as categorical as Schlegel. In an important essay in 1987, Martin Orkin accepted that there is "racist sentiment" in the play but says that it is largely confined to characters like Iago, Roderigo and Brabantio, whom the action thoroughly discredits – thus vindicating Shakespeare.

Jack D'Amico, in *The Moor in English Renaissance Drama*, finds this liberal view too comforting. Othello, he points out, does ultimately debase himself by submitting to the role Iago foists on him:

> To those in the audience who would await a return to his barbarous self, the altered behaviour merely confirms what the black visage promised, as the seemingly noble Moor becomes... the incoherent savage... The final paradox is that Othello is like everyone (particularly the European spectators) in his readiness to accept the negative, oversimplified stereotype of himself.

This may be true. Yet it is also true, as Michael Neill reminds us, that Shakespeare was writing in an age when the concept of racial difference simply didn't exist as it does now: the term "racism" wasn't even available to him, while the notion of

THE TRAGEDIE OF

Othello, the Moore of Venice.

Actus Primus. Scœna Prima.

Enter Rodorigo, and Iago.

Rodorigo.

Euer tell me, I take it much vnkindly
That thou (*Iago*) who hast had my purse,
As if y strings were thine, should'st know of this.

Ia. But you'l not heare me: If euer I did dream
Of such a matter, abhorre me.

Rodo. Thou told'st me,
Thou did'st hold him in thy hate.

Iago. Despise me
If I do not. Three Great-ones of the Cittie,
(In personall suite to make me his Lieutenant)
Off-capt to him: and by the faith of man
I know my price, I am worth no worsse a place.
But he (as louing his owne pride, and purposes)
Euades them, with a bumbast Circumstance,
Horribly stufft with Epithites of warre,
Non-suites my Mediators. For certes, saies he,
I haue already chose my Officer. And what was he?
For-sooth, a great Arithmatician,
One *Michael Cassio*, a *Florentine*,
(A Fellow almost damn'd in a faire Wife)
That neuer set a Squadron in the Field,
Nor the deuision of a Battaile knowes
More then a Spinster. Vnlesse the Bookish Theoricke:
Wherein the Tongued Consuls can propose
As Masterly as he. Meere pratle (without practise)
Is all his Souldiership. But he (Sir) had th'election;
And I (of whom his eies had seene the proofe
At Rhodes, at Ciprus, and on others grounds
Christen'd, and Heathen) must be be-leed, and calm'd
By Debitor, and Creditor. This Counter-caster,
He (in good time) must his Lieutenant be,
And I (blesse the marke) his Mooreships Auntient.

Rod. By heauen, I rather would haue bin his hangman.

Iago. Why, there's no remedie.
'Tis the cursse of Seruice;
Preferment goes by Letter, and affection,
And not by old gradation, where each second
Stood Heire to th'first. Now Sir, be iudge your selfe,
Whether I in any iust terme am Affin'd
To loue the *Moore*?

Rod. I would not follow him then.

Iago. O Sir content you.
I follow him, to serue my turne vpon him.
We cannot all be Masters, nor all Masters

Cannot be truely follow'd. You shall marke
Many a dutious and knee-crooking knaue;
That (doting on his owne obsequious bondage)
Weares out his time, much like his Masters Asse,
For naught but Prouender, & when he's old Casheer'd.
Whip me such honest knaues. Others there are
Who trym'd in Formes, and visages of Dutie,
Keepe yet their hearts attending on themselues,
And throwing but showes of Seruice on their Lords
Doe well thriue by them.
And when they haue lin'd their Coates
Doe themselues Homage.
These Fellowes haue some soule,
And such a one do I professe my selfe. For (Sir)
It is as sure as you are *Rodorigo*,
Were I the Moore, I would not be *Iago*:
In following him, I follow but my selfe.
Heauen is my Iudge, not I for loue and dutie,
But seeming so, for my peculiar end:
For when my outward Action doth demonstrate
The natiue act, and figure of my heart
In Complement externe, 'tis not long after
But I will weare my heart vpon my sleeue
For Dawes to pecke at; I am not what I am.

Rod. What a full Fortune do's the Thicks-lips owe
If he can carry't thus?

Iago. Call vp her Father:
Rowse him, make after him, poyson his delight,
Proclaime him in the Streets. Incense her kinsmen,
And though he in a fertile Clymate dwell,
Plague him with Flies: though that his Ioy be Ioy,
Yet throw such chances of vexation on't,
As it may loose some colour.

Rodo. Heere is her Fathers house, Ile call aloud.

Iago. Doe, with like timerous accent, and dire yell,
As when (by Night and Negligence) the Fire
Is spied in populus Citties.

Rodo. What hoa: *Brabantio*, Siginor *Brabantio*, hoa

Iago. Awake: what hoa, *Brabantio*: Theeues, Theeues:
Looke to your house, your daughter, and your Bags,
Theeues, Theeues.

Bra. Aboue. What is the reason of this terrible
Summons? What is the matter there?

Rodo. Signior is all your Familie within?

Iago. Are your Doores lock'd?

Bra. Why? Wherefore ask you this?

Iago. Sir, y'are rob'd, for shame put on your Gow

Y

race itself had more to do with lineage than with biology. It wasn't until full-scale involvement in the slave trade, and the expansion of the Empire in the late 17th century that theories of racial inferiority were properly developed in England. For Shakespeare and his contemporaries, as Neill says:

> the relationship between ethnicity and subordination was by no means clear; and Iago's continuing hints that there is something recognisably unnatural about the vesting of authority in the Moor are seemingly annulled by the Duke's public show of respect, and by Montano's deference ("'tis a worthy governor").

So Schlegel's view that Othello is a relapsing savage would probably have saddened Shakespeare. The play itself, as Neill says, constantly questions the significance of the protagonist's colour. Thus, while Iago's slurs in Act One, Scene One evoke the idea of unbridled black sensuality, it is Desdemona not Othello who speaks the language of passion when the pair of them are arraigned before the Senate, boasting of the "downright violence" of her feelings. Othello himself, as we have seen, is at pains to deny his "appetite".

When Iago talks of Othello as an "erring Barbarian" his words recall primitive fears of darkness and hark back to Old Testament passages like the one in which Jeremiah associates black skin with evil: "Can the black Moor change his skin? Or the leopard his spots? Then may ye also do good, that are accustomed to do evil." Desdemona, on the other hand, contradicts this stereotype, and the view expressed by her model in the Italian story, with her belief – based on another ancient theory of human development – that the torrid southern climate has burned up the hot and moist humours likely to cause jealousy, leaving the

AUDIENCE REACTIONS TO *OTHELLO*

Many anecdotes suggest *Othello*'s power to disturb audiences. Samuel Pepys remembered that when he saw it performed in 1660 "a very pretty lady that sat by me cried out to see Desdemona smothered". In the 18th and 19th centuries, people often wept openly. In 1746, Spranger Barry's Othello caused women to shriek in the murder scene. Half a century later Edmund Kean's performance made Byron cry, whilst, according to one account, "old men leaned their heads upon their arms and fairly sobbed". In a 1792 production in revolutionary France, "several of the prettiest women in Paris fainted in the most conspicuous boxes and were publicly carried out of the house". The man who had translated the play was so alarmed that he feared for his life and revised the play for subsequent performances, substituting a happy ending.

But while France had more than its fair share of hysterical audiences, the play's power to move was felt everywhere. In 1822, the French novelist Stendhal recorded an extraordinary event during an American performance: "A soldier who

African temperament cool, dry and melancholy: "I think the sun where he was born/Drew all such humours from him."

And, as Mary Floyd-Wilson convincingly argues, it is the white Iago's brooding inferiority and habitual suspiciousness that identify him with the naturally jealous temperament that the English were as likely to attribute to Italians as to Moors. So while it is undoubtedly the case that Shakespeare uses

---

was on guard duty inside the Baltimore theatre, seeing Othello... was about to murder Desdemona", intervened to protect her: "It will never be said that in my presence a confounded Negro has killed a white woman!" he shouted, and then fired his gun... breaking the arm of the actor who was playing Othello." A year does not go by, said Stendhal, "without the newspapers reporting similar stories".

In mid-19th century London, according to A.C. Sprague, even the relatively restrained Othello of William Charles Macready produced such a thrilling effect when he thrust his face through the curtains of the bed that a woman fainted at the sight. At another of his performances, when Macready seized Iago by the throat in the Temptation Scene, a gentleman "started up and exclaimed, loud enough for all around to hear, 'Choke the devil! Choke him!'"

As Michael Neill has pointed out, performers, too, have become caught up by the emotions of this play. In Freetown, Sierra Leone, in 1857, during a British military production, the commanding officer, who played Othello, shot his Cassio in cold blood, provoking a public scandal, while in 1942 Paul Robeson's adulterous affair with Uta Hagen, his second Desdemona and wife of his Iago, again made it seem as if the actors were being taken over by their roles.

Othello's colour to dramatic effect in the play, nowhere does he appear to suggest that his hero is in any way inferior because he is black.

But, if the modern emphasis on race in the play would have surprised Shakespeare, critics persist in it nonetheless. The American critic Karen Newman, for example, claims that the "marriage of a 'white' woman to a 'black Moor' is 'unthinkable' to all the other characters". This is misleading because it is not true – of Cassio, say, or the Duke, Montano and Lodovico. On the other hand, Newman's accusatory statement that "in the Renaissance no other colours so clearly implied opposition or were so frequently used to denote polarisation" is true but no less misleading, because, as we have noted, this statement is likely to be true of any culture at any time.

Does Othello regain his nobility in the final scene?

How much less lacerating – or less "unendurable", to use Dr Johnson's word – this play's final scene would be if we did not have to hear Othello making his own justifications, swinging to and fro in his unbearable agony, arraigning himself at one moment and then excusing himself in the next. His "soul" was "ensnared". His actions were not his actions. Could anything be worse than hearing him tell us what to think – "Nothing extenuate!" – and then having to hear him say that he was the one "who loved not wisely, but too well", while we are looking at Desdemona, dead?

What if she *had* been unfaithful? When Othello first confronts that question in his soliloquy in Act Three, Scene Three, his first, far more decent and loving response is that he would then turn her loose like a falcon, "whistle her off and let her down the wind/To prey at fortune". He would kick her out, not kill her. By the end of the scene, however, he is screaming for "Blood, blood, blood!" – both hers and Cassio's. After that, the issue for Othello is never whether to kill her, but how to kill her. The murder is not just premeditated; he is thinking of nothing else, for hours: "Get you to bed/On the instant", he tells Desdemona in Act Four, Scene Three, and "Dismiss your attendant there – look't be done." The murder is too carefully worked out to be a *crime passionel*, like that of Francesca's husband in Dante, when he finds her in bed with Paolo and skewers them both on his sword.

In the final scene Othello goes on and on insisting that he was right to kill Desdemona, until the moment when he is suddenly and with alarming ease convinced that she was innocent, after all. Before and after that moment he never once considers that murdering her would have been bestial, and anything but "noble", even if she had been unfaithful. Then he howls about what he has lost, his "pearl" and the like. As we noted earlier, both Coleridge and Bradley came shockingly close to suggesting that murdering Desdemona would have been perfectly compatible with Othello's awesome and majestic nobility, on which they endlessly insist, if only she *had* committed adultery. Of course neither explicitly makes such a shocking claim, but it is implicit in their insistence that the Noble Moor can regain his nobility in the final scene, once he realises that Desdemona was innocent. But do we believe that? Should we believe it?

I certainly do not believe, and cannot believe that Shakespeare believed, that killing an unfaithful or adulterous wife could ever be right, let alone "noble". On this matter at least, Leavis was entirely correct to protest against the whole English critical tradition of "sentimental perversity".

Nonetheless, the main line of English criticism from Coleridge through Bradley went on endorsing Othello's final view of himself in the final scene, that he (not Desdemona) was "one that loved not wisely, but too well", and that he was "one easily jealous, but being wrought,/Perplexed in the extreme". Even the renowned Shakespearean scholar A.D. Nuttall inclined to this extenuating view. In his last book, *Shakespeare the Thinker* (2007), he argues that Othello is not, or not necessarily, "completely deluded about his own nature" when he maintains that he was "not easily jealous". The point that then matters most for Nuttall, as for Coleridge and Bradley, is that the man who strangled Desdemona was "conceivably not the natural Othello but a substituted artificial man":

> The clue is in the word "wrought" in Othello's final speech – "but being wrought/Perplexed in the extreme." "Wrought" is often misused as if it were the past tense of the word "wreak". In fact it is the old past tense of "work" and is so used here. Othello is saying that he has been worked upon, wrought as a clay figure is wrought by the finger and thumb of the artist. He does not name Iago in the speech, but the sentence points at him and at no one else.

It does indeed, and that is what is so wrong. After the first shock and horror of realising that Desdemona was innocent, and that he had made a mistake, Othello takes refuge in his self-exonerating view of himself as the noble tragic victim whose "soul" was "ensnared" by a "demi-devil". He even dies believing that his grubby murder of some Turk in Aleppo was something to admire. He refuses to surrender his dream of an ideal Self. Every tortured playgoer feels for Othello, and would almost certainly think of the excuses that he makes on his own behalf – T.S. Eliot famously described his last speech as merely an effort to cheer himself up – but listening to him make the excuses is degrading.

We should recall, for example, what happens immediately after Emilia tells Othello that Cassio is still alive, and the bitterly disappointed Othello exclaims, like some composer aesthete:

> *Not Cassio killed?*
> *Then murder's out of tune, and sweet revenge*
> *Grows harsh. [5.2]*

The dying Desdemona then momentarily revives, and cries, "O falsely, falsely murdered". Quite so, but of course these are not her very last words, which we hear when Emilia opens the bed curtains, immediately calls for help, and begs her "sweet mistress" to speak again:

DESDEMONA:
> *A guiltless death I die.*

EMILIA:
> *O, who hath done*
> *This deed?*

DESDEMONA:
> *Nobody. I myself. Farewell.*
> *Commend me to my kind lord—O, farewell! [5.2]*

Desdemona then dies at last, after exonerating her "kind lord", whose immediate response is shamelessly self-preserving and anything but noble*:

> OTHELLO:
> *Why, how should she be murdered?*
> EMILIA:
> *Alas, who knows?*
> OTHELLO:
> *You heard her say herself it was not I.*
> EMILIA:
> *She said so; I must needs report the truth* [5.2]

Once his safety seems assured, Othello's next response suddenly flies in the opposite direction, but this too is anything but noble**:

> *She's like a liar gone to burning hell:*
> *'Twas I that killed her.* [5.2]

Othello then goes on and on insisting that "She turned to folly, and she was a whore", that she "was

---

* Of course the actor playing Othello can make this response in very different ways, as Michael Neill notes in his edition: "[Edwin] Booth, moved by Desdemona's speech, delivered this line as 'a half-choked utterance', whilst [Charles] Fechter spoke it with 'steady effrontery'."

** Pursuing the contrast between Booth and Fechter's performances, Neill notes that "Fechter's Othello showed 'a burst of triumph' here, where Booth registered 'deep emotion'." But, once again, none of these different theatrical possibilities is "noble".

as false as water", that "Cassio did tup her", that he himself "did proceed upon just grounds" to the "extremity" of murdering her, and that the "grounds" were "just" because Desdemona was covered by "the slime/That sticks on filthy deeds".

Nothing, it seems, will shake Othello's belief – and Coleridge's and Bradley's implicitly condoning belief – that murdering Desdemona would have been "just" or noble if only she had committed adultery. But the poor fellow was misled by Iago's "diabolic intellect". When Montano, Gratanio and Iago finally enter – 44 lines after Emilia's cry or scream for "Help, help, ho, help!" and 35 lines after Othello's admission "'Twas I that killed her" – the evidence of Desdemona's innocence multiplies, until Othello throws himself on the bed or marriage hearse crying, "O! O! O!" Has he at last realised what he has done? We wait in suspense, but when Othello gets up he is still insisting,

> O, she was foul.
> I scarce did know you, uncle: there lies your niece,
> Whose breath, indeed, these hands have newly stopped:
> I know this act shows horrible and grim. [5.2]

Not was and is, but "shows" or seems.

above: Poster for the premiere of Verdi's Otello, 1887

When Othello is still expostulating with Emilia in the final scene, he allows that

> *O, I were damned beneath all depth in hell*
> *But that I did proceed upon just grounds*
> *To this extremity.* [5.2]

Later, when Othello is finally – and so quickly – convinced of Desdemona's innocence, he longs for his own damnation, and even tries to ensure it, in Christian terms, by committing the allegedly mortal sin of suicide. His agony is then limitless. Of course we feel with him. But then we are forced to watch in horror as the poor wretch keeps swinging to and fro, until the very last, trying to ensure his own damnation – in Christian terms – by committing suicide, but trying to excuse himself as well. To understand is not necessarily, and sometimes necessarily not, to forgive. After some kinds of knowledge there is no forgiveness, and suicide is the only response for Othello as for poor, terrified Anna Karenina in her society. But Othello never stops prevaricating, even in his final speech.

The play is both a torture chamber and its remorseless Nuremberg trials aftermath. Nothing, and nobody, is spared, least of all the "Noble Moor".

What does *Othello* tell us about human happiness?

Verdi, who based his opera *Otello* on Shakespeare's play, liked to quote the old Italian proverb, "Fidarsi e' bene, ma non fidarsi e'meglio": *To trust is good, but not to trust is better*. One reply to this might be that the advice is excellent, but rules out happiness: there can be no happiness without love, and no love without trust. Iago's reply to that would probably be that, as Jonathan Swift wrote in *A Tale of a Tub*: "Happiness is the state of being perpetually well-deceived." *Othello* doesn't endorse any one of these three propositions, but it explores all of them.

The last proposition is the one Iago believes, and the differences between Othello and Desdemona are what he uses to "undeceive" them. Othello's race is the most important difference: it matters because he is an alien, and that gives Iago the vantage point from which to unpick the magnificent confidence in Othello's "She chose me": that's just it, Iago can then say, but *why* did she choose you, and what do you really know about Italy, or Venice, or women?

It wouldn't make much difference if Othello had been an Egyptian not a Moor; the idea of reversion to our more primitive selves is present in the play. The most relevant paragraph in Schlegel may make us wince now, especially when he writes of Othello assailing himself as a "runaway slave", but the paragraph is far more searching than anything Coleridge ever wrote about this play:

> The Moor seems noble, frank, confiding, grateful for the love shown him, and he is all this, and, moreover a hero who spurns at danger, a worthy leader of an army, a faithful servant of the state, but the mere physical force of passion puts to flight in one moment all his acquired and mere habitual virtues, and gives the upper hand to the savage over the moral man. This tyranny of the blood over the will betrays itself even in the expression of his desire of revenge upon Cassio. In his repentance, a genuine tenderness for his murdered wife, and in the presence of the damning evidence of his deed, the painful feeling of annihilated honour at last bursts forth, and in the midst of these painful emotions he assails himself with the rage wherewith a despot punishes a runaway slave. He suffers as a double man, at once in the higher and the lower sphere into which his being was divided.

Schlegel's slave metaphor is not his own invention; he is taking it directly from the final scene – and his discussion of Othello's "divided being" makes even better sense in terms of contemporary cognitive science, which has shown how our experience of "self" is always split. What is happening in the final scene, in cognitive terms, is that Othello-the-Subject is at last confronting and acknowledging the one of his selves which he calls a "cursed Slave", and which he had tried to disown in the crucial "Had it pleas'd Heaven" speech. At last – but only spasmodically (like Lear or Coriolanus) and in the most tortured way – Othello sees this other "Self" as part of the metaphorically constructed "Me". So, before he executes himself, he calls for his own damnation: "O cursed, cursed slave! Whip me, ye devils... Blow me about in winds, roast me in Sulphur." But then, in this excoriating play about "Self"-deception, he starts prevaricating again, in his all too familiar and all too human way. He can't blame the "fair devil" Desdemona any more, so he swings back to blaming the "demi-devil" who "ensnared" his "soul".

As George Orwell observed of Lear's final but never more than spasmodic moments of illumination, there is no steady progress, and no final illumination. But there has been a fitful kind of progress from what Othello could not even acknowledge in his counterfactual "Had it pleas'd Heaven" speech. The cognitive approach to this tragedy is more helpful than any other because it entails that we must recognise ourselves in Othello, and his own foundational fictions, or illusions, about who or what he is. Modern cognitive science holds that the so-called Self is always split and is always ineluctably metaphorical – a construct. So, like Othello, we all have a succession of different selves and to a greater or lesser extent we can be transformed into something we might hardly recognise, as he was.

In Othello's case, the change is more extreme because he is an idealist (as is Desdemona – they are both idealistic in disastrously different ways). In the end, it is as if he is taken over by Iago's nihilism. In a 1991 essay, the critic Joel Fineman points to the strange lines spoken by Iago in the first scene: "Were I the Moor, I would not be Iago" and "I am not what I am". Othello and Iago, he suggests, are complementary: Iago is inside Othello.

Shakespeare's understanding of the idea of the fractured Self is not so surprising, since he pressed our language further and in more directions than any other writer, but it is yet another example of the way he anticipated modern psychological ideas. In the last 30 years, cognitive linguists have shown how the distinction between Subject and one or more Selves (as in phrases like "I'm not myself" and "I've let myself down") is present in our every linguistic utterance about the "Self".

Towards the end of *A la recherche du temps perdu*, Marcel Proust's narrator Marcel suggests that one finds one's self only as a succession of "selves": "On ne se réalise que successivement." A similar idea emerges – more playfully but no less unforgettably – in a BBC *Goon Show* script, when Minnie is complaining, as usual, to her husband Henry:

MINNIE:

You're not the man I used to know.

HENRY:

Who was the man you used to know?

MINNIE:

You were the man I used to know.

HENRY:

I'll get even with him!

WHAT THE CRITICS SAY

There is in this play some burlesque, some humour, and ramble of comical wit, some show, and some mimicry to divert the spectators... the tragical part is plainly none other than a bloody farce, without salt or savour.
[Thomas Rymer, A *Short View of Tragedy*, 1693]

Let me repeat, Othello does not kill Desdemona in jealousy, but in a conviction forced upon him by the almost superhuman art of Iago, such a conviction as any man would and must have entertained who had believed Iago's honesty as Othello did.
[Samuel Coleridge, 1813]

[Othello's love] may be love, but it can only be in an oddly qualified sense love of her: it must be much more a matter of self-centred and self-regarding satisfactions – pride, sensual possessiveness, appetite, love of loving – than he suspects.
[F.R. Leavis, "Diabolic Intellect and the Noble Hero", *Scrutiny 6*, 1937]

Everybody must pity Desdemona, but I cannot bring myself to like her. Her determination to marry Othello - it was she who virtually did the proposing - seems the romantic crush of a silly schoolgirl rather than a mature affection: it is Othello's adventures, so unlike the civilian life she knows, which captivate her rather than Othello as a person.
[W.H. Auden, "The Joker in the Pack", *The Dyer's Hand*, 1962]

The most painfully exciting and the most terrible of all Shakespeare's tragedies.
[A.C. Bradley, 1904]

The Moor seems noble, frank, confiding, grateful for the love shown him... and, moreover a hero who spurns at danger... but the mere physical force of passion puts to flight in one moment all his acquired and mere habitual virtues, and gives the upper hand to the savage... In his repentance... he assails himself with the rage wherewith a despot punishes a runaway slave. He suffers as a double man, at once in the higher and the lower sphere into which his being was divided.

> [A.W. Schlegel, "Criticisms on Shakespeare's Tragedies", *Lectures on Dramatic Art*, 1802]

For all its "superficiality and staginess, [Othello] remains magnificent by the volume of its passion and the splendour of its word-music, which sweep the scenes up to a plane on which sense is drowned in sound. The words do not convey ideas: they are steaming ensigns and tossing branches to make the tempest of passion visible... Tested by the brain, it is ridiculous; tested by the ear, it is sublime."

> [Bernard Shaw, quoted in Edwin Wilson (ed), *Shaw on Shakespeare*, New York, 1961]

[The] dark essence of Iago's whole enterprise... [is] to play upon Othello's buried perception of his own sexual relations with Desdemona as adulterous.

> [Stephen Greenblatt, *Renaissance Self-Fashioning*, 1980]

What Othello seems to me to be doing in [his last] speech is cheering himself up. He is endeavouring to escape reality, he has ceased to think about Desdemona, and is thinking about himself... I do not believe that any writer has ever exposed this bovarysme, the human will to see things as they are not, more clearly than Shakespeare.

> [T.S. Eliot "Shakespeare and the Stoicism of Seneca", *Selected Essays*, 1953]

A SHORT CHRONOLOGY

1564 Shakespeare born in Stratford-upon-Avon.

1565 Giraldi Cinthio's *Gli Hecatommithi*, or *A Hundred Tales*, containing *Un Capitano Moro*, the source for the plot of *Othello*. The tales also provide the source for *Measure for Measure*, and for Beaumont and Fletcher's *The Custom of the Country*. There was no English translation; some who doubt that Shakespeare could read Italian have suggested that he read the 1583 French translation by Gabriel Chappuys.

1570-73 the Turks take Cyprus from the Venetians, after which they dominated the eastern Mediterranean, even after a heavy defeat by a Christian navy at the Battle of Lepanto in 1571. A 1600 charter gave 83 merchants a monopoly on English trade to Venice, a major trading rival, and Turkey.

1599-1600 *Hamlet*.

1603-4 *Othello*.

1604 first performance of *Othello* before James I's court, in the Banqueting Hall at Whitehall Palace.

1605-6 *King Lear, Macbeth*.

1612 *Othello* is one of twenty plays performed in celebration of the wedding of James I's daughter, Elizabeth, to the Elector Palatine in the winter in 1612.

1616 Shakespeare dies on the 23rd April.

1693 Thomas Rymer's *Short View of Tragedy* scorned *Othello*, which fell short of his neo-classical standards, dismissing it as the "Tragedy of the Handkerchief": "This may be a warning to all good Wives, that they look well to their Linnen."

1816 premier of Rossini's *Otello*.

1819 Coleridge's lectures on *Othello*.

1887 Verdi's *Otello* opens in Milan.

1904 A.C. Bradley's *Shakespearean Tragedy*, concurs with Coleridge's judgment of Othello as "the noble Moor".

1931 Paul Robeson appears as Othello, opposite Peggy Ashcroft and Ralph Richardson, the first black Othello since Ira Aldridge in the 19th century.

1937 F.R. Leavis's publishes his essay, "Diabolic Intellect and the Noble Hero".

1946 W.H. Auden's "The Joker in the Pack".

1952 Orson Welles directs, stars in and finances a production of *Othello*.

1964 Laurence Olivier and Maggie Smith star in a controversial National Theatre production of *Othello*.

1980 Stephen Greenblatt's *Renaissance Self-Fashioning*.

BIBLIOGRAPHY

W.H. Auden, "The Joker in the Pack" in *The Dyer's Hand and Other Essays*, Faber, 1963

Harry Berger, *Imaginary Audition: Shakespeare on Stage and Page*, University of California Press, 1989

A.C. Bradley, *Shakespearean Tragedy: Lectures on "Hamlet", "Othello", "King Lear" and "Macbeth"*, 1904 (reprinted by Penguin, 1991 with a foreword by John Bayley)

Jack D'Amico, *The Moor in English Renaissance Drama*, University of South Florida Press, 1991; stems from the author's teaching experiences in Lebanon and Morocco; covers Dekker, Heywod, Johnson, Marlowe and Middleton as well as Shakespeare's Othello, Aaron and King of Morocco.

Mary Floyd-Wilson, *English Ethnicity and Race in Early Modern Drama*, CUP, 2003

Stephen Greenblatt, *Renaissance Self-Fashioning*, Chicago University Press, 1980; classic of New Historicist criticism.

G.K. Hunter, *The Oxford History of English Literature: English Drama 1586-1642*, OUP

Jan Kott, *Shakespeare Our Contemporary*, Methuen, 1964

F.R. Leavis, "Diabolic Intellect and the Noble Hero", 1937, re-printed in *The Common Pursuit*, Chatto and Windus, 1952

Ania Loomba, *Shakespeare, Race and Colonialism*, OUP, 2002

Michael Neill, *Othello, the Moor of Venice*, OUP, 2006

Karen Newman, *Essaying Shakespeare*. University of Minnesota Press, 2009

Karen Newman, *Fashioning Femininity and English Renaissance Drama,* University of Chicago Press, 1991

Charles Nicholl, *The Lodger: Shakespeare on Silver Street*, Allen Lane, 2007; biography charting Shakespeare's life as a tenant of the Huguenot Mountjoys, during which he wrote *Othello, Measure for Measure* and *All's Well that End's Well* as well, Nicholl claims, as persuading the Mountjoys' apprentice to marry their only daughter.

A.D. Nuttall, *Shakespeare the Thinker*, Yale University Press, 2007; takes a more dynamic view of Shakespeare's thinking than most historicist criticism, tracing the themes of motivation and personal identity through the plays.

Edward Pechter, *Othello and Interpretive Traditions*, University of Iowa Press, 1999; a close reading focusing on the play's formal qualities, over feminist, post-colonial or historicist readings; distinctive on Desdemona and Bianca, downplays Iago.

INDEX

122

First published in 2010 by
Connell Guides
Short Books
3A Exmouth House
Pine Street
London
EC1R 0JH

10 9 8 7 6 5 4 3 2 1

Picture credits:
p 16 © Bettmann/CORBIS
p 29 © British Home Entertainment/Warner bros/ The Kobal Collection
p 84 © DaTo Images
p 109 © Lebrecht Authores

A CIP catalogue record for this book is available from the British Library.
ISBN 978-1-907776-00-7
Design © Nathan Burton
Printed in Great Britain by Butler Tanner and Dennis Ltd, Frome